GET
BETTER
GRADES

GET BETTER GRADES

Cool Study Skills

for Red Hot Results

Piccadilly Press • London

Phototypeset from author's disk by Piccadilly Press.
Printed in Great Britain by St Edmundsbury Press Ltd., Bury St Edmunds, Suffolk
for the publishers Piccadilly Press Ltd.,
5 Castle Road, London NW1 8PR

A catalogue record for this book is available from the British Library

ISBN: 1 85340 310 5 (trade paperback)
1 85340 305 9 (hardback)

Margie Agnew lives in Hammersmith, London. She is a teacher in a
Comprehensive school and has been involved in Study Skills courses
for students and training courses for teachers.

Steve Barlow lives in Heanor, Derbyshire. He has worked in a wide
assortment of jobs but finally settled on teaching. He has written
several books in collaboration with Steve Skidmore for Piccadilly
Press including I FELL IN LOVE WITH A LEATHER JACKET, IN LOVE
WITH AN URBAN GORILLA and a series, THE ADVENTURES OF BW
– BOOKWORM.

Lee Pascal lives on a boat. He lectures on Writing and
Study Skills in secondary schools. He is also a Special Needs teacher
with a particular interest in Dyslexia.

Steve Skidmore lives in Leicestershire. He spends his time teaching,
writing and watching Leicester Tigers. He met Steve Barlow while
teaching in Nottingham and they began writing together.

Reprinted 2000

CONTENTS

INTRODUCTION

So, you want better grades?

nfortunately, there is no easy way to pass exams, **BUT** we hope to give you lots of tips about how you can use your study time more effectively. We'll do this by giving you techniques and tips that you are not always told at school.

Get Better Grades is a **DIP-IN** book. Don't read it from cover to cover. You may wish to look up a certain topic – how to write essays for instance. Look this up in the contents page (or the index). Then turn to the appropriate pages and see what pearls of wisdom you can glean! There are SEE ALSO boxes which give you further references to sections that are related to each other.

IMPORTANT POINT!

DO <u>NOT</u> JUST READ THIS BOOK.

Although *Get Better Grades* will give you superb advice, great tips and fantastic study skills, the book isn't as important as the person reading it and that person is **YOU.**

It is you who have to put them into practice and apply them to your work. If you do, we're sure that you will improve your performance and your study skills. But, to get better at something, you have to practise!

We've tried to make the book fun and enjoyable because it is our belief that you learn better when you are enjoying yourself!

So over to you – **HAPPY STUDYING!**

ATTITUDE

SHOCK, HORROR! TEACHERS ARE HUMAN!

Latest research has discovered the fact that teachers are HUMAN!

After years of painstaking observation, evidence has revealed that teachers
- have emotions
- have families
- pay bills
- laugh
- cry
- go to the toilet
- sometimes moan about having to get out of bed early in the morning in order to go to school.

But perhaps the most startling fact of all is that teachers WERE ONCE TEENAGERS and went to SCHOOL!

This incredible information can be used to a student's advantage!

A famous scientist* explains:

By knowing that teachers are human, we can predict how they will react in certain situations. This enables us to be able ultimately to control their behaviour and use them for our own purposes.

Contrary to all previous belief, it has been discovered that teachers are USEFUL!

*Well, nearly famous. **
** All right, not famous at all.

8

A famous scientist★★★ explains:

Teachers are one of the best resources a student can have. They will know what the student should be learning and thus be tested

We tried these experiments on teachers.

What happens to a teacher if a student sits like this throughout a lesson?

on in exams. They should know how well the student is doing. They will be able to tell students the correct facts and where to find them. And they also offer practical advice and encouragement. All in all, they are incredibly useful and should be used properly by students!

Result
The teacher got pretty fed up teaching this person. The student was obviously bored and taking no interest. Because the teacher is human, they got annoyed and angry with this student and developed a "not bothered" attitude back to the student.

★★★Not the same as the last one.

But what happens if the ▲ student sits like this?
Result
The teacher felt good about this person and wanted to do well for this student. They even wanted to give them extra help!

Another famous scientist**** states:

These results may be summed up in the scientific human equation:

For every ACTION there is a REACTION.

If you act well towards a teacher, they will act well towards you. If you act badly, then expect some sort of bad reaction back! **Better Grades** TOP TIPS for dealing with teachers:

• Don't act badly towards them – you never know when you might need their help!

• Don't sit at the back of the class all the time – they'll wonder why you don't want to sit near them!

• Be enthusiastic and interested – they'll want to do their best for you.

• Give them a smile, every now and then. If nothing else, they'll wonder what you're up to!

**** (Okay that's enough famous scientist jokes, Ed.)

SEE ALSO PAGES 21,40,50

11

SEE ALSO PAGE 22

🦌 RECIPE TIME 🦌

Just follow this quick and simple RECIPE for success. Motivation is a great dish for those days when you're sitting down, wondering "Why on earth have I got to do this piece of boring work!"

It's easy to make, but few students try it out. It will help you to develop a positive state of mind and give you one or more reasons for succeeding.

MOTIVATION

Ingredients
1 bored student (possibly you)
A set of exams to pass
Lots of schoolwork
Paper, Pens

Method
1. Take the student.
2. Make them think about why they want to succeed and what goals they have for themselves.
3. Take paper and pen and write down these reasons and aims, e.g. I want to be a millionaire; I want to go to university to study medicine; I want to be independent of parents and bosses.
4. Pin this up next to the student's desk or on their bedroom wall.
5. Make the student look at it at regular intervals (especially when they are really struggling over a piece of boring schoolwork).
6. Maintain at a constant temperature over a period of time.

By the time exams and tests arrive, the student should be ready to serve with a crisp side salad and a glass of mineral water. *Bon appétit!*

SEE ALSO PAGE 16

EDUCATION

Who is responsible for your education?

a) The Government
b) Teachers
c) Parents
d) Yourself
e) Your pet

ANSWER: (d)

You are responsible for your own learning and education. It is up to you to make sure that you have as much learning as possible.

WHY?

To be able to achieve what YOU want to achieve from YOUR life.
It isn't up to governments, parents or teachers; the responsibility lies with you. So don't make excuses if things are not as you would wish them to be. Take action to make them better.
Remember:

IT'S YOUR LIFE – BE RESPONSIBLE!

THOUGHT FOR THE DAY

I keep six honest serving men,
They taught me all I knew,
Their names are What and Why and When,
And How and Where and Who?

From *The Elephant's Child* by Rudyard Kipling

Questioning is INCREDIBLY important in studying. It makes you become more active. If you just take in information all the time, it will quickly fade away. By asking questions that YOU are interested in, you have given yourself a way of concentrating because your mind will be looking for answers.

How can I use this information?

What is the point of doing this?

Why does the writer say this?

Where can I find out further information?

Questioning keeps you focused on your task by making it relevant to you.

P.S. AWFUL JOKE

Do you like Kipling?
I don't know, I've never Kippled!

NOTABLE QUOTABLES

Henry Ford knew a thing or two about state of mind and success. He believed that negative thoughts produced negative results and positive thoughts produced positive results.

"Whether you think you can – or whether you think you can't – you're probably right."

He also said:

"They can have any colour as long as it's black,"

but that was about the Model T Ford motor car and isn't really relevant to a study skills book!

"Genius is 99 per cent sweat and one per cent talent."
(Edison)

SEE ALSO PAGES 11,12,22

GET DOWN!

It is said that to be a writer you need paper and pen (or nowadays a computer, printer and paper) and a pot of glue. The pot of glue is needed in order to stick your bottom to a chair. This is the only way that you will stop yourself from getting up every two minutes in order to avoid doing any writing.

This is exactly the same as getting down to studying. Once we do manage to get down to some work it's okay (well, okayISH), but it's the getting down that's the hardest.

It's useful to recognise the tactics you use to avoid finishing the essay that has to be handed in, or the revision that you should be doing in order to pass your exams. So here to help is the Better Grades Guide to Excuses.

You know you're putting off work when you find yourself doing one of these:

USUAL EXCUSES FOR PUTTING OFF WORK

Making cup of tea
Making cup of coffee
Making cake
Reading magazine
Reading book (not to do with
  what you should be doing)
Phoning boyfriend
Phoning girlfriend
Phoning anyone at all
Making another cup of tea
Trying on new trainers
Trying on new dress
  (put this under Desperate Excuses if you are male)

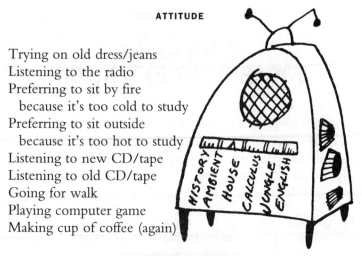

Trying on old dress/jeans
Listening to the radio
Preferring to sit by fire
    because it's too cold to study
Preferring to sit outside
    because it's too hot to study
Listening to new CD/tape
Listening to old CD/tape
Going for walk
Playing computer game
Making cup of coffee (again)

DESPERATE EXCUSES

If you have ever used any of these excuses, you are a very sad creature:

Ironing your clothes
Ironing all the family's clothes
Any form of cleaning
    like dusting, washing pots,
    tidying bedroom, etc.
Picking fleas from
    dog/cat/goldfish/budgie
Listening to parents' tapes/records
(e.g. Status Quo, Buddy Holly,
    Gary Glitter, etc.)
Offering to go shopping
Going trainspotting
Having a sensible
    conversation with your parents

SEE ALSO PAGE 12

Better Grades
VOCABULARY EXTENSION

PROCRASTINATE pro-kras'ti-nat, v.i. to put off action, to delay; ns procrastination, a putting off till a future time: dilatoriness: procrastinator. [L. procrastinare – pro, onward, crastinus – cras, tomorrow]

Day of the Week	Subjects set	Subjects done	Emotional response
Monday	French, Maths, Geography	French	Resentment. Better things to do.
Tuesday	Maths, Geog, English	English & bit of Maths	Not prepared to think about this hassle.
Wednesday	Maths, Geog, Biology, French, English, Chemistry	Geography	Furious with Mum, she never stops going on at me.
Thursday	Maths, Biology, Eng, Chemistry, French and History	Maths & more maths	Now Dad's having a go.
Friday	EVERYTHING!	None done	Thank God it's Friday!
Saturday		None done	Out till late
Sunday		Badly: Maths, Bio, Chemistry, English, French	PANIC! HYSTERIA! DEPRESSION!

HAS THIS EVER BEEN YOU?
WHAT COULD YOU DO ABOUT IT?!

SEE ALSO PAGES 98,101

HEALTH AND FITNESS TIPS

GET YOUR BRAIN INTO SHAPE!

Yes, Summer's coming and it's time for exams! But are you ashamed to take your brain into an exam hall? Do you look around that hall thinking there are better looking, fitter brains? Do you wish that you had the sort of brain that attracts others?

Well now's the time to get your brain into shape with our terrific tips for shaping up for Summer, Spring, Autumn and Winter to make sure you're ready for exams all year round!

Don't be ashamed of your brain!

Like all complicated machinery your brain needs energy to make it tick – but it needs the right sort!

We get our energy from food, so a sensible diet is important. The brain needs glucose, sodium, iron and potassium to help it get into tip top condition. These are found in fresh fruit and vegetables (bananas are especially rich in potassium). Some experts also say that lecithin is very important in helping improve memory. This is found in soya beans and wheat germ.

The brain also needs oxygen. Exercise helps to get oxygen into your blood and enrich your brain. So do some exercise to help get your brain in shape!

Smoking is very bad for the brain – it deprives it of oxygen. Alcohol is also not so good! It can destroy brain cells.

It helps to do deep breathing exercises before studying or going into an exam.

TONE THAT MUSCLE
It is important to keep your brain toned up all the time. You may not be studying for exams constantly, but your brain needs stimulating if it's going to shape up. Try reading a novel, doing puzzles, playing chess or perhaps playing a computer game. Do whatever you find fun!

Better Grades TOP TIPS
● Eat a good breakfast every morning. Try to include fresh fruit.
● Eat a good lunch which includes plenty of salad/vegetables.
● Make fish, nuts and vegetable fats a key part of your diet.
● Try to avoid "junk food".
● Exercise regularly to put oxygen into your blood.

IN A NUTSHELL
Sensible eating and exercising will help you become proud of your brain.

PS It will help you to look great on the beach as well!

DEAR BRENDA

Have you got problems with schoolwork, parents and life? Well don't sit there fretting and worrying about them; share them with Better Grades award-winning agony aunt, Brenda.

Dear Brenda,
My history teacher is a real prat. He's got B.O. and he doesn't know how to teach. The class is always messing about and he gets really leery. He has been piling on the work in the last few weeks and is picking on me because I'm a little behind in my course work.
He says I'm thick and lazy and will fail my exams. I feel like walking out of his class and giving up history altogether. Why should I work for such a nerd?
Louise

Dear Louise,

I hate to be the one to break the news to you, but YOU'RE the nerd!

I guarantee you that in three years' time if anyone were to ask your history teacher how Louise got on, his reply would be "Louise who?". You're not getting back at him by not doing the work or by leaving his class. He would prefer you to succeed but if you fail it WON'T affect HIS life.

Wouldn't it feel great to know that even though he was such an awful teacher, you did succeed and proved him wrong. Get real Louise. Finish your course work, study hard for the exam and then wave your results in the nerd's face!
Brenda

SEE ALSO PAGES 8,40,50

Dear Brenda,
I know that I should be working and I'm getting really brassed off with everyone telling me to get on with it and study hard. People have been telling me what to do all my life and I'm getting fed up with following orders.
I feel like dropping out of school and telling them all to get lost. Why should I bother with exams when I know that I can get a job straight away and stop having to do what I'm told all the time?
Darren

Dear Darren,

It's because you want to stop taking orders that you should stay on at school and get some exams under your belt. It's generally true to say that the more qualifications you have, the fewer people there are above you to give you orders. At the moment you have very little control of your life, and if you give up now you'll always have people telling you what to do. Get some qualifications and they will help you to be your OWN boss.
Brenda

SEE ALSO PAGES 11,12

ORGANISATION AND RESOURCES

WHAT SORT OF WORKER ARE YOU?

There is no such thing as the perfect student. We all have different talents. But it is best to know our strengths and weaknesses in order to be able to concentrate on the areas that need improving.

Try this Better Grades quiz to help you identify those areas of study that could do with improvement. Jot down your answers on a separate piece of paper, then check them against our answers to find out what sort of worker you are!

1. Do you work from a weekly/monthly planner?
   a) A what?
   b) No, never.
   c) Sometimes, if I remember or can be bothered to.
   d) Usually, except when I forget.
   e) Yes, always – aren't I good!

2. Do you always have everything you need (books, pens, etc.) to hand before you start to study?
   a) I never study.
   b) No, I always have to keep getting up to get something I've forgotten.
   c) Not as often as I should.
   d) Usually – I'm a fairly organised person.
   e) Yes always – I'm so organised that my nickname is Filofax.

3. Does your place of study (desk/room) look tidy?
   a) I can't get into my room to my desk as it's so messy.
   b) Yes, if I move those underpants and dirty socks, oh and those papers,magazines and books and...
   c) Yes, after mum has cleaned my room up by throwing everything on to the landing.
   d) Usually – it's fairly tidy most of the time.
   e) Of course – even the sun has to wipe its feet before being allowed into my room!

4. Do you have enough study equipment at hand such as files, highlighters, paper, dividers, index cards, etc?
   a) What are they?
   b) Not really ...
   c) Yes, when I can persuade the parents to buy me some.

d) Usually, except towards the end of term, when I run out.

e) Yes, in fact WH Smith come to me for their supplies.

5. Do you review your notes and handouts at regular intervals?

a) What notes and handouts?

b) Yes, at a regular interval – once a year.

c) Maybe every term – depends if I'm bored.

d) Usually, maybe every half term or so ...

e) Of course I do, doesn't everyone!

6. Do you ever use any memory techniques to help you memorise your work?

a) What are memory techniques?

b) I can't remember.

c) Sometimes when I remember to.

d) Quite often. It helps me to remember important things.

e) Yes, always. I practise by remembering the phone book!

7. Do you plan your essays?

a) I don't write essays.

b) No, I just write my ideas down as I go along.

c) Sometimes, when I'm reminded to.

d) Usually – it helps me know what I am going to write.

e) Yes. I plan them out to the tiniest detail.

8.Are you confident about your spelling?

a) Ov coorse I yam.

b) Not really. It can be a bit ~~doddgy dogdy~~ bad.

c) It's okay, although I sometimes make "silly mistakes".

d) Yes, it's pretty good.

e) It is perfect! I have written a dictionary.

9. Have you ever tried "shared" note taking and note making?

a) No, 'cos I don't take notes.

b) No, I do it all on my own.

c) I have once or twice.

d) I usually do.

e) All the time. I have an extensive network of friends who share notes.

10. Do you find it easy to identify KEY words in your notes?

a) I just told you, I don't take notes.

b) No, I have great difficulty.

c) Sometimes; it depends what the words are!

d) I'm fairly good at spotting the key elements in my notes.

e) Of course!

11. Have you ever practised different reading techniques for different tasks?

a) What are you on about?

b) Isn't there only one way to read?

c) I think I have.

d) I use skimming.

e) Yes, I use scanning, skimming, and read essay questions very carefully.

12. Do you read your work before handing it in?

a) I never hand in work.

b) No, it's too boring!

c) Sometimes, if I'm not in a rush to hand it in.

d) I usually do – it helps me to spot any errors.

e) Always, because what I write is so interesting!

13. Do you read exam questions or titles of essays carefully?

a) Yes please, but no sugar in mine.

b) No, and I often get bad marks because I don't answer the question.

c) Sometimes I do.

d) Nearly always.

e) Always – it is important to know what you have got to write about.

SCORES

a) = 0 points

b) = 1 point

c) = 2 points

d) = 3 points

e) = 4 points

Add up your score for questions 1, 2, 3 and 4.

These questions are designed to show how organised you are.

0 points: Uh oh! You are totally disorganised. It's a wonder that you can get out of bed and get dressed! (Quick, make sure you've managed to put some clothes on!) By being in a muddle all the time, you are not using your study time to the best advantage. You have to be organised in your approach to studying if you wish to achieve your best.

1-5 points: You are someone who could do with some organisation in your study life! By being organised, you can actually save yourself time by having things to hand because you know where they are. This means that you'll get your work done in less time and have more time for LEISURE. Get organised – it's worth it!

6-10 points: Not bad, but try to spot where some organisation could help you to achieve EFFECTIVE use of your study time. Once you've spotted this, put it into practice!

10-15 points: You are obviously a well organised person. This gives you a definite edge when it comes to getting better grades. If there are one or two areas that you could "tighten up" on, try to do something about it.

16 points: INCREDIBLE! Are you by any chance a robot? You are so organised that people could set their watches by you!

SEE ALSO PAGES 18,32,98,101

Add up your score for questions 5 and 6.
These are to do with revision.

0 points: Forget about better grades, you'll be lucky to get any grades! You must make notes, keep them organised and look over them at regular intervals. Turn immediately to the section on revision, before it's too late!

1-3 points: You need to brush up on revision techniques and put them into effect straight away. Otherwise you could be the one in the exam who is sitting staring at the clock, wishing the exam would end because you can't think of anything to write!

4-7 points: Not bad, but try to make sure that revision is a large part of your study time, especially as you get closer to exams. Maybe you should brush up on one or two memory techniques.

8 points: Incredible, but don't waste time on remembering the phone book!

SEE ALSO PAGES 101,103

Add up your score for questions 7 and 8.
 These are to do with essay writing.

0 points: I think you've got a problem here! You'd better read the relevant sections in this book and then get help from your teachers QUICKLY!

1-3 points: This is an area that you need to spend some time on. It is a vital skill if you are going to get better grades. Look up the relevant sections on essay writing for some worthwhile advice.

4-7 points: Not bad, but there's still some room for improvement – even professional writers learn more about writing as they get older!

8 points: Are you sure you're answering these questions truthfully?

SEE ALSO PAGES 63,66

Add up your score for questions 9 and 10.
 These are to do with note taking.

0 points: Are you ever at school and if you are, what do

you actually do all day? Please read the relevant sections on note taking IMMEDIATELY!

1-3 points: It is important to make worthwhile notes in order to be able to revise well for the exam. Good notes are essential for better grades, so read the advice on page 56 and start making notes that are going to help you!

4-7 points: Not bad. You should try to read through your notes often and make sure that you understand everything in them.

8 points: I'm fed up with telling you how wonderful you are!

SEE ALSO PAGE 52

Add up your score for questions 11, 12 and 13.
    These are to do with reading skills.

0 points: I'm afraid that you need help quickly!

1-5 points: Reading is probably the most important skill. It is essential that you practise the different types of reading if you are going to get better grades. If you don't know what these are then look them up in this book.

6-11 points: There are some areas in reading skills which you could brush up on. It is important to realise how advantageous it is to use the different types of reading skills in order to maximise your efforts.

12 points: It is obvious that you have superb reading skills and apply the different techniques when you need them. Congratulations!

SEE ALSO PAGES 60,62

DEAR BRENDA

Dear Brenda,
It is impossible for me to study for my exams. I get home after school and the house is full of brats screaming all over the place. I have to share a room with my older sister and she just sits around smoking with music blaring away. I can't concentrate and I'm way behind with my course work. I feel like giving up and getting on the welfare like her.
Tina

Dear Tina,

It sounds as though you've picked a pretty poor role model to base your life on! You've started off really badly by giving yourself excuses for failure. Now get your act together and look for reasons to succeed! A look at your sister should give you enough reasons to do well in your exams.

Who says that you've got to study at home anyway? There's probably a library nearby and you've got friends at school with quiet houses to work in. Maybe your school can let you stay on for a bit after classes, or perhaps you've got a relative who would be happy to let you drop by and use their house. Come on Tina, BE POSITIVE. Get out of your failure zone and look for a place to succeed!
Brenda

SEE ALSO PAGES 11,15,32

SPOT THE DIFFERENCE

How many differences can you spot in these two pictures?

Did you spot the difference? Which picture is nearer to how your study space looks? Which do you think is the ideal study space?

You may not be able to achieve a study space that even remotely resembles picture B, but if your study area looks like picture A then you may have a problem!

If it isn't possible for you to arrange a suitable area for study, perhaps you could use the local library or even a relative's house.

B.

THE *Better Grades*
TOP STUDY BOOKS

Reviewed by Buck Werm

1. *A Dictionary*
This is an essential book for everyone. It's suitable for all ages and can help with spellings and meanings of words. It's a MUST for any serious student!

2. *A Thesaurus*
Here's another essential book for the serious student. It is a book of words that is arranged according to ideas and meaning. It will help you to find alternative words and help you increase your vocabulary. The most famous thesaurus is *Roget's* which has over 250,000 words and phrases. An excellent volume for finding alternative words to use instead of "nice"!

3. *A One-volume Encyclopaedia*
There are several of these on the market – you can even get them on CD ROM! They are incredibly useful for looking up facts for projects, etc. Perhaps the most famous is the *Pears Cyclopaedia*.

4. *A Multi-volumed set of Encyclopaedias (e.g. Encyclopaedia Britannica)*
Wow! If you can afford these then they really are worth every penny. Mind you, you might prefer to go to a library to use them and spend the money you save on a holiday!

5. *A Biographical dictionary*
Very useful for finding out all about dead famous people. (The people in it are usually dead and famous!)

6. *An atlas*
Just to help you know where on Earth everything is!

7. *A Year Book*
There are lots of these about nowadays – they have up-to-date information about a whole variety of things. They are excellent for providing facts and figures for project work.

8. *The Guinness Book of Records*
For all those facts that you really don't NEED to know but are fun anyway!

9. *A Guide to English (e.g. Oxford English)*
A book like this is excellent for giving you tips about spellings, grammar, "tricky words", technical phrases and pronunciation. Some even give you quotations and a guide to famous writers and their works. A great book.

10. *A Foreign Language Dictionary*
C'est très bon, ooh la la!

11. *A Chronicle of the 20th Century*
An excellent book for keeping in check with the last hundred years. Vital for history students and anyone with an interest in the world (which means you!).

12. *A Dictionary of Quotations*
Brilliant for peppering your essays with good quotes or finding out who really said what!

13. *A Study Skills Book*
THIS ONE!

WISH YOU WERE THERE!

Have you got time to spare? Want a break from studying? Or do you just want to have some fun?

Well, here's the Better Grades guide to top hot spots to visit that can help your studying and put you on the path to getting better grades!

THE LOCAL LIBRARY

A tip top hot spot. It's THE place to hang out for useful information! Books, magazines, newspapers, records, videos ... oh yeah, and you might meet a like-minded student, know what we mean!

MUSEUMS & ART GALLERIES

These are brilliant places. Nowadays, more and more museums have hands-on displays and interactive exhibitions. Much better than the old "look-but-don't-touch" approach. Most major cities have several museums. Check them out for info and fun!

HISTORICAL RE-ENACTMENTS

There are events happening every week in some part of the country. From small-scale events to large historical re-enactments. This is a great opportunity to see history come alive. Some-where near you, you can be guaranteed to see knights jousting, Victorians being schooled, minstrels singing or battles being fought.

LOCAL INFORMATION & TOURIST OFFICES

Obviously you don't want to spend a whole day in one of these, but find a local one and try and visit it at regular intervals in order to keep up with what's on.

HISTORIC HOUSES, CATHEDRALS, & CASTLES

You don't have to just wander round these being bored. Try and imagine what it would have been like to have lived in them, what sort of people lived there – what famous historical events happened there? The list is endless. Go on, be brave, enjoy yourself!

NATIONAL TRUST PROPERTIES

There are hundreds of these all around the country. From moors, cliffs and gardens to castles and abbeys, there's something for YOU!

TV STUDIOS & NEWSPAPER OFFICES

If you're interested in the media, it would be worth trying to arrange a visit to see how news and television programmes are created. Ask your teacher about the possibility of organising a trip.

FACTORIES & OFFICES

Many factories and offices are willing to take people around and some have open days. It is an opportunity to look at the world of work – to give you ideas about your future career or just to gain information about the business world.

THEATRES & CINEMAS

Good for English exams! Enjoy yourself whilst studying! What could be easier!

OTHER COUNTRIES

Family holidays can be a source of education. Experience different lifestyles and customs. Perhaps your school operates a foreign exchange scheme. Useful for helping with your foreign language n'est-ce pas?

SEE ALSO PAGE 40

MULTIMEDIA
WAYS OF LEARNING

n this high tech age it's important to be up to date with the latest technology.

TEKNO TEZ is here to guide you through the uses of multimedia!

Right you floppies, put away those Super Mario games, Street Brawler 57 and that dopey hedgehog, it's time to use your computer to help you get stonkin' good grades!

Personal computers are essential! It's the age of the chip, and I don't mean soggy battered potatoes. PCs are here to help YOU, so get real and TAKE ADVANTAGE! They are everywhere: libraries, schools, homes, you name a place and there's a silicon chip hiding somewhere! Use them for getting INFORMATION!

CD ROM is a truly excellent information storage and retrieval device. These little silver beauties contain a heap of information. From whole encyclopaedias to an interactive visit to a museum, these are

THE FUTURE

and you heard it here first! Oh yeah, and you can even see video clips and listen to the computer telling you the info! Unbelievable! But be careful or the Terminators are gonna take over!

PCs can help you with projects: you can use them as word processors and for Desk Top Publishing – making your work look mega ace. Spreadsheets are a doddle, maps can be reproduced, and some software packages allow you to present graphs in any shape, form or size you choose! You might even check out the Internet and start surfin' those electronic waves.

GET INTO THESE THINGS SOONEST!

But come on TEK what else can I use to help get better grades? Glad you asked.

Television is always useful – and not just for watching Australian soaps – there are documentaries and news programmes that will inform you. Videos are relatively low cost and there's a HUGE selection of these; from top-selling films to period costume dramas, there's bound to be some vids that can help you with your set books and plays!

Radio is also okay and not just the MUSIK stations – try some of the talking stations – they have discussions, documentaries and even SCHOOLS programmes. You should find something to help you.

Oh yeah, don't forget newspapers and magazines from nationals to specialist mags. There are loads of these, and whether it's *Canal and River Boat Monthly* or *Beekeeping Weekly*, there is bound to be something that could help you. And you don't have to buy these – get down to the library and give them a look. Tek says: *For better grades, get into multimedia.*

SEE ALSO PAGE 34

SPOT THE PERSON

Which of the following could help you to get BETTER GRADES?

MUM

DAD

friends

teacher

GRANDPAR

UNCLE

journalist

LIBRARIAN

an author

PET

PARROT

PET

MOUSE

YOURSELF

AUN

ENTS

shopkeeper

Answers on the next page!

Who can help you to get better grades?
ALL OF THEM!
Make the most of anybody who could help you. They are resources for your education and learning!
They might:
● have specialist knowledge
● give help with information for projects
● suggest ideas
● give you different viewpoints
● pass on their experiences
● discuss your ideas
● test you
● help you with some typing
● provide you with materials
● give you information (businesses might give you project packs)
● photocopy information.

Think of one way that each of these people could help

YOU!

Don't forget that you are an important resource too because of:
● the knowledge you have
● travel you may have undertaken
● visits to historical houses etc
● your own experiences
● questions you ask yourself and want to answer.

And how could the parrot and mouse help?

They could be a resource for a science project or an art project. But please try to avoid using them in cookery projects!

SEE ALSO PAGE 36

STRANGE BUT TRUE

It was the morning of Sue's GCSE Maths exam. Unfortunately she got up late as she forgot to set her alarm clock. Not only was she rushing about trying to get dressed, brush her teeth, do her make-up AND eat breakfast at the same time, she also had to get her exam equipment together. This was because Sue hadn't got these items ready the night before, as she thought she would have plenty of time in the morning to pack her pens, pencils, rulers etc.

Sue rushed about the house, yelling at everyone and blaming her mum, dad, sister, dog and budgie for not waking her up.

She got her writing implements together, but couldn't find her calculator. This was a totally essential item – she'd never be able to work out some of the problems without it.

Again she yelled at everyone (and everything – including the goldfish) before she saw the calculator lying on the floor in the lounge. She threw it into her pencil case and shouted at her sister for daring to touch it and then leaving it lying around on the floor where anyone could step on it.

Luckily, Sue's mum offered to drive her to school and Sue arrived just in time for the exam. Sue entered the exam hall, sat down, breathed a huge sigh of relief and opened up her pencil case. She took out her six pens, pencils, her ruler, the packet of mints and her good luck gonk. She then reached in to pull out her calculator. As she pulled it out she gave a cry of horror.

Instead of looking at her expensive calculator that was going to help her pass her GCSE Maths exam, there in her hand was the zapper for the television!

AAAAGGGHHHHH!

Better Grades SHOPPING LIST

Ever thought of how to get some cash out of your mum or dad willingly?

Try this: tell them you have just read this book and you need all these things to help you study and enable you to get better grades!

file dividers
hole puncher
blu-tack
plastic wallets for files
plain paper
lined paper
graph paper
highlighter pens
pen
ruler
coloured pencils
felt tips
ink cartridges
index cards
calculator
diary/planner

index file box
sellotape
stapler & staples
computer discs
clipboard
school bag, if necessary
paper clips
pencils
paper adhesive
ring reinforcers
templates
sticky labels
corrector fluid for
    emergencies
eraser
ink correction pen

Then BUY them! (If your parents can't afford some of the items, try and borrow them!)

WHAT DOES THE FUTURE HOLD FOR YOU?

Do you need to ease up and give yourself a break?
Do you want to reduce your study time and get better results?
Help is at hand!
We've asked our very own special study skills astrologist, Clarence, to look into his crystal ball to help you!

Read the horoscopes and see if you can find solutions to your problems in your and other people's star signs.

ARIES
(March 21–April 20)

You're strong willed, have a great sense of humour, and are a born leader. When you are not leading, you prefer to be on your own to sort out your own problems.

Beware Aries! Working on your own may mean that you are missing out on the help that other people can give. Try STUDYING and REVISING with a friend and see how much faster you can learn the material.

One last thing, Aries: don't let your natural lively sense of humour turn into cheekiness in your exams. Some fuddy duddy examiners hate cheekiness and regard it as insolence! So don't give them a chance to take marks off you!

SEE ALSO PAGES 40,103

TAURUS
(April 21–May 21)

You really are just like the proverbial bull in the china shop!

You tend to rush into things without planning or thinking of the consequences. You MUST read over your exam questions and then give yourself a minute or two to settle down and compose yourself.

Spend some time PLANNING your answers. Also, don't be put off by the idiot sitting at the table next to you who has written half a page by the time you have finished reading the questions; he's the one who will have his pencil stuck halfway up his nose in the middle of the exam trying to think of what to write next!

SEE ALSO PAGE 114

ORGANISATION AND RESOURCES

GEMINI

(May 22–June 21)

What a star you are! You're quick thinking, get great ideas but seldom follow them through. You're the one we turn to for getting started on a project but, unfortunately, you soon get bored and move on to something else.

You're also the one who gets "You haven't stuck to the point" and "This essay hasn't been planned" written at the bottom of your papers.

When it comes to exams, Gemini, PLANNING is ESSENTIAL if you want to stop yourself losing marks.

SEE ALSO PAGE 66

CANCER

(June 22–July 23)

Oh boy, aren't you the cautious one! Not only that, you're also MOODY and tend to look to others and blame THEM for YOUR lack of success. Stop this immediately and take responsibility for your own learning! Start right away and organise a study timetable. DON'T let others put you off sticking to it. Look for reasons to succeed, not for excuses for failure.

You're capable, bright and can achieve the marks you want. Do it!

SEE ALSO PAGES 11,13

LEO
(July 24–August 23)

Roar! Yes, that's you – a real rip-roaring lion, courageous and impulsive! These qualities can be great assets when approaching your exams. BUT you have a tendency to rush straight into writing your answers down without reading the questions carefully and giving yourself time to sort out and PLAN what you're going to say.

You're the sort who comes out of exams, and when discussing the exam with friends, slaps yourself on the forehead and cries out: "Oh no! Were we really supposed to answer four from section one and three from section two?" Read the questions through carefully, imagining that you are the examiner, and you will save yourself a major amount of grief.

SEE ALSO PAGE 121

VIRGO
(August 24–September 23)

You are methodical and you have a good memory. Perhaps you don't FEEL that you remember things all that well, but have you explored the different memories that you can use? One of them will be successful, so now is the time to explore. Instead of staring at your notes to try to memorise them with your eyes, try dictating them to a tape recorder or reading your notes aloud so that you can use the memory of your ears. Perhaps writing things down, using the memory of your hand, will be successful. How about helping your memory by colour coding your notes? Yes, Virgo, you have a super memory. Now all you have to do is find out which one it is. And then USE it!

SEE ALSO PAGES 57,90

LIBRA
(September 24–October 23)

You're a terrific listener and are very involved in trying to sort out the problems of those around you. However, you sometimes get so wrapped up in other people's problems that you tend to disregard your own, or keep them bottled up. If you are experiencing difficulties in studying, or if you are feeling exam panic, DON'T keep it to yourself. Let your teachers know and tell your friends about your worries. You may have been approaching your studies from only one angle, and other people may be able to share study secrets and exam techniques with you. Go on, ask them and see how other people can help YOU!

SEE ALSO PAGES 8,40

SCORPIO

(October 24–November 22)

Yes, you certainly have the traits of the Scorpion and I don't mean that you sting people to death! You have a great capacity for planning and calculating for your success, so use this skill wisely, and plan your essays with care. However, like the Scorpion, you tend to dash from subject to subject and not give yourself enough time to absorb information.

When you study for exams, try to have a five/ten minute break every forty minutes. When you return to your books, go over the information that you were working on before the break. Then after ten minutes revision of this work, you can go on to something new.

SEE ALSO PAGE 103

SAGITTARIUS
(November 23–December 21)

Yes, Sagittarius, you get straight to the point and have set high standards for yourself. However, you are a strong individual and are reluctant to take advice from those around you. Don't be so stupidly headstrong! You need to trust the expertise of your teachers more and take note of those comments at the bottom of your essays. Pay attention to these and act on them — and see your marks get better and better! Try making a list of the teachers' comments, and then use these remarks as a check list when you plan your essay.

SEE ALSO PAGES 8,40

CAPRICORN
(December 22–January 20)

What a star! You are committed and can work away at a task for hours at a time. Once you have set your mind on something, you are very reluctant to break away from your goal. This is an excellent attitude, Capricorn, but give yourself a break! Remember, all work and no play can actually LOWER your marks. When athletes are resting, they don't consider this period as wasting time; they are regenerating the system and and allowing their batteries to charge up.

Make sure that YOU allow some time for recreation in your study diary, and ease up on the long periods without a break.

SEE ALSO PAGE 98

AQUARIUS

(January 21–February 19)

Aquarius, you are both methodical and calm – you have a tremendous capacity for organisation and preparation before starting any task. But BEWARE! Time might run out on you while you are still planning your strategies. You have a tendency to spend hours planning your study schedule and then run out of time for the actual studying! Be careful too, when in an exam. Try to use a quick and easy method for outlining essays, otherwise you'll run out of time.

SEE ALSO PAGE 67

PISCES

(February 20–March 20)

Yes Pisces, we know: you're the life and soul of every party! You're popular, witty and will happily stay out until three every night and forget about the less pleasant sides of student life. Sorry Pisces, if you care about taking control of your life instead of spending the rest of it being told what to do, you're going to have to do a bit of investing now in the form of hours and dedication. These may not be the best years of your life. In fact, for you to be successful, these study years will probably be stressful, pressured and at times AWFUL!

Cheer up though, Pisces. If you handle your study years correctly, you'll have all the resources you need for the rest of your life to be as happy and stress free as you want to make it!

SEE ALSO PAGE 111

DEAR BRENDA

Dear Brenda,
I find that note taking is a real bother with me spending hours and hours trying to get everything down on paper as the teacher is talking, well not exactly everything but most of what she says in history and all of what he says in English because it's so important and I feel that if I leave anything out I won't get a good grade in my exams and I will be so disappointed because I really want to go on and do a course in business studies and I realise that I'm up against some pretty stiff ...
Annie

Dear Annie,
I managed to get to your name by skipping through all that drivel and getting to the end of your three-page mini series. If your note-taking is as wordy as your letter, you're in REAL trouble. It is important to take down some of your teachers' pearls of wisdom, but try using your ears as much as your pen and you may find that you can write really useful study notes.

Listen especially hard at the beginning and at the end of the lesson as the teacher will often give outlines and summaries of his/her lesson. Use abbreviations and short phrases rather than sentences. If you can knock a phrase down to one or two words, so much the better. Above all, keep your notes brief.
Brenda

SEE ALSO PAGE 57

LISTENING AND NOTE-TAKING

Signal Words

Some words that teachers and lecturers use when speaking to a class are "signal words", a sort of code that indicates you should pay special attention. If you're sharp and pick them up, you could save yourself a lot of grief! If you're not ... kiss your pass goodbye!

Marvellous Maxine thinks...

The Speaker says:

Viv the Div thinks ...

He said four reasons – he wouldn't list them if they weren't important, so I'd better note them down...

"There are four reasons... "

What's he on about? Four what? Four seasons? Ooh I couldn't half fancy a pizza...

... if I've got to keep it in mind, I'd better make sure I remember it!

"Keep in mind..."

I've got to keep in mind the fact that Mark's packed Carole in so he's available, yum yum!

Examples are useful because they show that what's being said is correct. When I hear words like these, I know that the stuff that follows will support what I write so I'd better remember it.

"As an example..."

"For instance..."

"Also..."

"Plus the fact that..."

There are about a hundred things I'd rather do than listen to this, for example getting a new hair-do, for instance going out with Mark, plus the fact that I can't remember what he just said.

What if someone asks awkward questions about what I've written? I need to know the arguments against, and comparisons, so when I hear these words I need to take notice of the points that may be raised against me!

"However..."

"Nevertheless..."

"Equally..."

"Likewise..."

Mark's a bit dim, however he's quite dishy. Our teacher's quite cute. Nevertheless, he's dead wrinkly. I've lost the thread of this. Equally, I don't understand it. Likewise, I can't be bothered.

Words like this show that the speaker is going to summarise what they've said, so now's a good chance to make sure I've understood it all and not missed anything.

"Thus..."

"To conclude..."

"These facts show us..."

"Finally..."

Connie WHO? Oh right, good, he's going to finish. Well get on with it then. I'm starving. Where's my bag? If I pack up now, I can be first in the queue for dinner. I can save a seat for Mark.

Oh-oh! This is code for "remember this, or else!" Especially if they say it twice! It could mean we'll be asked questions on this stuff later.

"Listen carefully..."

"Remember this..."

"The important points you need to know are..."

Come on, come on, remember what? I don't remember a thing. Questions? On what we've learnt? What have we learnt? Next week?!

EVER COME OUT OF A LESSON WITHOUT A CLUE WHAT THE TEACHER HAS JUST SPENT 45 MINUTES BABBLING ON ABOUT? IF YOU HAVE YOU SHOULD:

TAKE NOTE!

WHY TAKE NOTES DURING LESSONS?

1

70 per cent of what we hear, we forget.

2

Taking notes helps us to focus and listen.

HOW CAN YOU PREPARE YOURSELF?

1

Sit near the front.

2

Sit away from Distracting Dave or Doris.

3

Have the right equipment.

TAKE NOTE!

HOW DO YOU KNOW WHAT IS IMPORTANT?

1

Listen for signal words (see page 53).

2

Listen and ask questions if you don't understand.

WHAT ARE YOUR AIMS?

1

To pick out the key points.

2

To keep tests and exams in mind.

3

To provide yourself with a set of revision notes.

How Do You Brain Frame?

Easy! Follow these instructions:

BRAIN FRAME INSTRUCTIONS

Write or draw the main topic or theme in the middle of the page – turn the page horizontally to give you more room.

Think about the **KEY** words.

Write these down, branching out from the main idea. You should also use pictures or symbols to represent these words.

Think about the theme or topic. Add new ideas or thoughts you may have.

Redraw your Brain Frame. Organise it into ideas that go together or add lines to connect these ideas.

TIPS

Make the Brain Frame as visual as possible. Use colour, symbols and pictures – the brain will remember these more easily than just words.

Use capital letters in order for words to stand out. Leave space – if you clutter up the page your brain won't take in as much information.

Use the Brain Frames as posters – stick them up on your walls, in the loo etc.

A BRAIN FRAME OF A BRAIN FRAME!

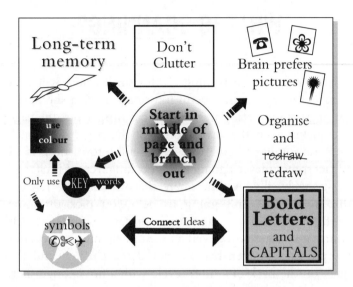

TRY IT OUT!

Topics you could try:

Then get on to your subjects.

DON'T FORGET TO PRACTISE BRAIN FRAMING

NB: Brain Framing is also known as *"Mind Mapping"*, *"Learning Maps"* or *"Spidergrams"*.

SEE ALSO PAGE 101

READING SKILLS

WHAT IS SCANNING?

There's no point in reading all this small print, as it isn't going to give you any useful information. You should be reading the important message by **scanning** across the page and picking out the main points of the page. This small print isn't going to give you any useful information, **is** it? In fact sometimes it's going to repeat itself, repeat itself, and be strangely silly. **A** fish. There that was silly. So reading this small print isn't going to help you pick up some **method** to help you in your important exams is it? **Of** course not. There isn't even a joke to help me in **covering** the **pages**, not even the one about the chicken **and** the duck on the back of a motorcycle with a fire extinguisher. Have you noticed that there aren't two **paragraphs**, only one? You had? Well you're a clever one. I bet you finish exams **quickly**. So why are you persisting **in** reading this totally useless drivel? **Search** me! What a lot **of** time you have to waste as **the** most interesting thing on this page is...well there isn't one! There must be an **answer to** why you're still reading this. Well, **one** can't sit here all day. But what else could I be doing? Now that's a good **question**, **i.e.** I could be abroad, in Greece for instance, or **looking** at an historic Roman site. Of course **for** something else to do, I could be visiting a museum looking at **one** masterpiece by Manet with its amazing **detail** and colour. **Or** in **fact** I could be lying on a beach. I'd rather be anywhere than writing this. I can't believe I'm having to waste my time writing it, but if **it's** proving a point and helps you to pick up **an important reading technique**, then I suppose I'll have to. So what's the weather like today in your neck of the woods? "Your neck of the woods" that's a fairly stupid idiom **we use**, isn't it? You might not live anywhere near a wood. Isn't **this** true? And why should your neck be anything to do with it? I'm trying to use anything, any **method** to try and finish this. **When** is it going to finish? When can **we** turn move on? **Are** you bored yet? So what was the weather **looking** like yesterday? Here it was raining. No, tell a lie, it's sunny today, it was raining yesterday, and I got wet. Very wet. "Weather fit **for** ducks", as my gran would say, but I ask you has anybody asked a duck if it actually likes rain, and if they have, has a duck ever replied? The answer is of course, no, never! There are **a number** of other things I need to include **in** this paragraph, but I'm running out of space. Oops, there's **the telephone**. Must go. You can get on reading the rest of the **book**.

Did you read all of this or just the words that stood out? Well, scanning is all about picking out important words, not reading every word. It is a reading technique that helps us to save time and find information – FAST!

HOW TO SCAN

1. Decide WHAT you are looking for and in what form it will most likely appear in print, e.g. a name or a statistic.
2. Scan for appropriate clues. Capital letters to locate names, numbers to pinpoint statistics.
3. Try to focus on what you are looking for. Don't be distracted by other words or pictures. Only the likely clues should come into focus, the other words should be hazy. ➤ ➤ ➤ ➤ ➤ ➤ ➤ ➤ ➤ ➤ ➤ ➤ ➤

SKIMMING

Skimming is another important reading skill.
It is a method of getting the whole picture and then picking out selected portions. It is a useful method if you are trying to find out if a book is likely to contain any relevant material.

The purpose is to read only the KEY sentences and KEY words that are likely to give us the relevant information.

HOW TO SKIM

1. Read the title, introductory remarks and table of contents.
2. Read the first paragraph which REALLY introduces the chapter. Don't pay attention to irrelevant material.
3. SURVEY the whole chapter.
4. Read the first sentences of each paragraph. Try and anticipate what clues it gives you about the nature of the rest of the paragraph.
5. Scan to pick up KEY WORDS in the paragraph.
6. Read the last sentence of the paragraph.
7. Read the concluding paragraph of the chapter.
BE FLEXIBLE – if the paragraph isn't providing you with the information you want, skip it!

IMPORTANT: Because Skimming means that you are having to select and analyse what you are reading, it needs a high level of concentration!

➤ ➤ ➤ ➤ ➤ ➤ ➤ ➤ ➤ ➤ ➤ ➤ ➤

WRITING SKILLS

The
Better Grades
Essay Spotter

We turn to Dickie Rottenburra for his help in spotting the several species of essay that exist in the world:

Here in the vast expanses of the academic world, otherwise known as school or college, there are several species of essays, lying in wait for the unsuspecting student.

One can only wonder at the subtle but very differing types of essay that bait the student before... CRUNCH, the student is trapped and wondering how they have been so stupid to allow an essay to catch them out.

Some essays are more common than others. The lesser spotted discursive essay is particularly abundant in the summertime, when thousands of students can be seen sitting in exam halls trying to feed these voracious creatures with paper and ink.

Less common perhaps is the hook-clawed investigative essay, which takes a lot of time in trying to research what its feeding habits are.

Nevertheless, with training and careful research and thinking, students will soon be able to spot these different species of essay.

DISCURSIVE ESSAY:	**An essay which involves discussion and argument.**
Example:	Should all schools have a uniform?
Tips:	Make a list of advantages/disadvantages, for/against, pros/cons, use quotes from other books/sources.
FACTUAL ESSAY:	**An essay which requires knowledge of the subject.**
Example:	Dinosaurs.
Tips:	Be clear about which are facts and which are opinions.
INVESTIGATIVE ESSAY:	**This type of essay requires experiments, surveys, exploration.**
Example:	How would the building of a nuclear power station near your town affect the local community?

| *Tips:* | Research thoroughly before starting to write. Design realistic questionnaires. Draw conclusions from these. Ask for opinions as well as researching facts. |

| **NARRATIVE ESSAY:** | **This type of essay involves telling a story. It includes descriptive passages and feelings and emotions have to be expressed.** |

| Examples: | My worst day ever! |

| *Tips:* | *Only write from personal experience, and involve all the senses (see, feel, smell, hear, taste and believe!). Don't tell us the main character has brown eyes (most people have blue or brown eyes!). And don't ever rehash dreams!!* |

WRITING PLANS

FLOW DIAGRAM

This plan is particularly useful for humanities essays and creative writing.

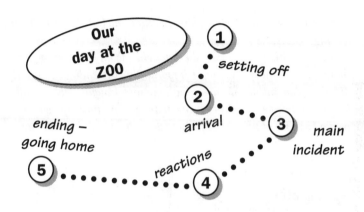

SIDE BY SIDE

This form is used for compare and contrast essays, or for those which ask for an opinion. Compare and contrast your ideas side by side in columns.

E.G.

Essay title:

"Smoking should be banned in public places." Discuss.

FOR	AGAINST
Passive smoking	Impinges on freedom
Filthy pollution	Causes stress to smokers
Odour	Cut sales (jobs at risk)
Fire risks	Attraction of forbidden
Setting bad example	What next to be banned?

LINEAR PLAN

This is a useful alternative to the Flow Diagram and can also be used to list ideas and expand on them. In a creative plan, think of the end, the beginning and then the middle, fill in the topics, headings 1, 2, 3... Then fill in the subheadings a, b, c...

This is the plan that Marvellous Maxine made before she began writing her story.

Before writing the plan she thought about the setting, the characters, the story and, most importantly, the ending. Not only did this plan cut out an amazing amount of awful flabby waffle, it saved Maxine hours of sitting with a pen stuck up her nose, trying to think of what to say next while she was writing the story.

OUR DAY AT THE ZOO
1. Setting off
a) Intro, mention disaster
b) Kevin whingeing
c) Jalopy

2. Arrival
a) Juicy description of Millie
b) Kev and me bored
c) Feel sorry for the animals

3. Main Incident
a) Set up – mention Millie's hair
b) Millie leans forward
c) Elephant grabs wig

4. Reactions
a) Us laughing
b) Millie hopping about
c) Millie covering her real hair

5. Ending
a) Wig spat back
b) Millie humiliated by keeper
c) Drive home & end sentence

Creative writing includes
– stories
– descriptions of people
– descriptions of places.

You should always try
– to make your writing interesting
– to create an atmosphere
– to describe what your characters think and feel.

One of the first things you have to decide when writing a story is whether you are involved in it (in which case you will write things like "I saw" and "I did") or whether you are outside the story looking in (so you would write, "he saw" or "she did").

When you've read these stories, try reading Maxine's story and Viv's, changing all the "I"s and "we"s to "she"s and "they"s. What effect does this have?

HERE'S MAXINE'S TERRIFIC STORY!

OUR DAY AT THE ZOO

Our day was supposed to be a treat, but it nearly ended in disaster.

When Aunt Millie invited us, we weren't very keen to start with. As Kevin said, "Who wants to spend all day looking at mouldy animals?" Nobody wanted to hurt Aunt Millie's feelings though, so we clambered into her battered jalopy and set off.

It was a grizzly grey day, and Kevin and I felt pretty droopy, but Aunt Millie never takes any notice of the weather. She bustled about on stumpy legs, peering short-sightedly at the labels that tell you all about the animals, saying things like, "My, my!" and "Well, I never." Kev kept hinting that he was hungry, and I said perhaps we could go to the cafe for a sit down, but Aunt Millie wasn't listening. She never does. We were getting more miserable by the

WRITING STORIES

• *Try using a short, punchy first sentence to grab the reader's attention.*

• *Try to use accurate nouns and verbs. "Clambered" is more interesting than "got" because it suggests that getting into the car was difficult, and "jalopy" shows that Aunt Millie's car is old and battered.*

• *Maxine tells us about Aunt Millie by*
– describing her physically
– mentioning things that make her different from other people
– telling us what she does.
How does Maxine do this, and what sort of impression does this give us of Aunt Millie? Do you think you could draw a picture of her?

• *What people say is important because it tells the reader a lot about them. Why does Aunt Millie keep saying "My, my!" and "Well, I never"? What does this tell the reader about her?*

minute. I felt sorry for the gorillas that look at you with the great sad eyes, and the snakes in the reptile house made me feel creepy.

It was all a dead loss until we went into the elephant house.

Now, one of the things we found strange about Aunt Millie was that no matter what she was doing, she never had a hair out of place. We used to ask Mum about it, but she'd just go quiet and change the subject.

You're not supposed to feed the elephants, and Aunt Millie didn't mean to, but while she was reading the label that told you all about Indian elephants and saying "My,my!", one of the elephants reached out with its trunk and grabbed Aunt Millie by the hair.

Kev and I were frightened at first that Aunt Millie might be hurt, but the elephant simply lifted Aunt Millie's hair

- *Maxine tells the story of what happened. This is the narrative. But she also tells us about the people in the story and their surroundings. This descriptive writing is mixed up with the narrative to keep the reader's interest, and together the narrative and description create an atmosphere.*

- *What is the climax of the story?*

- *Maxine doesn't change tenses from past to present or back again! What tense does she use?*

- *Maxine's story has only one main incident in it. Does this matter?*

- *There is a lot of narrative towards the end of Maxine's story. She describes the climax of the visit and what happened afterwards.*

right off her head and started waving it about! It was a wig!

We couldn't help laughing. Aunt Millie was hopping from foot to foot, squeaking, "Bad boy!" at the elephant as if it was a big naughty dog, and trying to cover her real hair (which was grey and mousey) with her hands.

Luckily, the elephant didn't like the taste of the wig and spat it out. A keeper handed it back, with a lecture about not feeding the animals that had Aunt Millie seething with rage.

We felt very sorry for Aunt Millie, but we had to work very hard at not giggling as we drove back. Aunt Millie stared very hard at the road ahead and said nothing.

It'll be a long time before Aunt Millie forgets our day at the zoo!

• *What is Maxine's role in the story?*

• *How does Maxine invite the readers to feel part of the story?*

• *Include the title in the last paragraph of the story. This rounds the story off neatly by reminding the reader of what it was all about.*

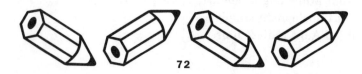

NOW READ VIV'S ACCOUNT OF HER TRIP TO THE ZOO

It was great at the Zoo, it was a school trip for Environmental Studies, we went on a coach and we sang songs on the back seat and Val was sick three times.

Mr Peck got mad and told us to shut up and we did for a bit but then we started making rude noises but he pretended not to hear.

When we got to the zoo we went and looked at the penguins and Jason started to walk like a penguin, it was a great laugh, then we all went in the cafe for a cola and crisps. I thought the animals were nice, except the wallabies, it said wallabies on the cage but we never saw them, I don't think there were any in there, but most of the animals were really nice, especially the koala bears, they were dead cute, and the monkeys were nice,

• *This opening sentence is trying to do far too much. It says what sort of trip it was, why Viv went, how she went, what happened on the journey; this is far too much for one sentence! It is important in creative writing to be selective. This means that you pick out the incidents that help the story along. Viv is writing down everything she can remember, but not using it to tell a story.*

• *Why does Jason imitate a penguin? Why is this funny? Viv doesn't tell us enough, so it's difficult to imagine the scene. This shuts the reader out.*

• *Viv doesn't exactly tell us anything about the animals or how they make us feel, they are all "nice", "cute" or "boring". This doesn't help the reader feel a part of what's going on either.*

too, I wanted to take one home. The crocodiles were boring though, they never did anything, they just lay there, I recokon they were stuffed ones, it was a con.

Then we went to look at the polar bears and Ian leant right over the wall to see them in the water, he leant so far he nearly fell in, Kelly had to grab his jacket or he would've fallen over and probably got eaten, but we went to see the seals being fed the keeper threw a fish to a seal and it tried to catch it but only knocked it up in the air and it hit Kelly in the face and Ian laughted at Kelly which wasn't very nice after she'd probably saved him from being eaten by polar bears and she was crying and after that we went home.

• *There's so much going on in this story, it's hard to keep pace. There's high jinks on the bus, Jason and the penguins, Ian and the polar bears, Kelly and the seals; Viv doesn't tell us which is most important, so how can we know?*

• *The main trouble here is that it sounds a really interesting and exciting trip that Viv is describing, but because she tries to tell us everything that happened and doesn't give us any details about anything, we can't get involved in it.*

• *The story isn't rounded off, it just stops, as if Viv has got fed up with writing it.*

WRITERS' MASTERCLASS

**Problems with creative writing?
Limp plots, weak narrative?
Dangling participles?
Dame Jennifer Archery
is here to help!**

I wrote this mega brill essay about this robot from the future that was sent back to kill someone so his grandson wouldn't get born and it could turn into anyone or anything and it was an ace essay but my teacher gave it Z minus, what should I do?

Dame Jennifer replies:

I'm not surprised your teacher gave you Z minus! Your story sounds very much like the "Terminator" films to me.

Don't rehash film plots for your essays – teachers watch films too, you know! Anyway, it's not your work and it won't look convincing to a reader.

Don't try to find "exciting" plots. People write absolutely terrible stories about mad scientists trying to blow up the world and the hero arriving in the nick of time etc; on the other hand, some of the best stories I know are just about ordinary people trying to make sense of life.

Don't write about "dream" sequences either; it's almost impossible to do well because dreams only seem to make sense when you're dreaming. Try telling someone else about your dream and they'll think you're weird.

Write on!

My friends always seem to be able to think of stories when our teacher sets essays; I can never think of any! Where can I find good ideas for creative writing?

Dame Jennifer replies:

The best stories are often those written from personal experience, especially when you're dealing with things that mean a lot to you, or that you or the person you're writing about feel strongly about.

A lot of people make the mistake of trying to cram too many ideas into one essay. If you're only asked to write 400–500 words, you haven't space to play around with lots of different ideas – writing about one thing clearly and in detail will give you a much better story. And always remember that you're writing this story for someone else to read!

Write on!

My girlfriend says she likes my plots but she finds my characters flat and boring. I am worried because she has started saying things like, "I couldn't respect a boy whose characters aren't really rugged". How can I make my characters more rugged (and keep my girlfriend)?

Dame Jennifer replies:

I don't know about rugged. If all your girlfriend is interested in is rugged characters I suggest you buy her a book on carpet-weaving and go out with someone else.

When you're planning a character, the reader will be interested in:

– what the character looks like

– what makes the character special and different from everybody else.

You can do some of this through description, but the things your character says and does can tell the reader just as much and will probably be more interesting!

Write on!

I find planning my essays really difficult. By the time I get to the end of my plan, I've usually wandered so far off the point I can't even remember what the title was. Help!

Dame Jennifer replies:

This may sound daft, but the best way to plan is usually back to front! In other words, you START with the ending, then go to the start and work your way back through the middle.

You'll find this method a bit hard to begin with, but stick with it – it's a great way of making sure you stick to the point.

Write on!

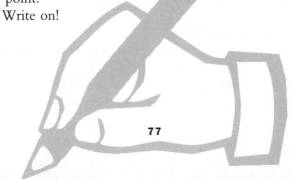

77

My English teacher says I must use more metaphors and similes. What is he on about?

Dame Jennifer replies:
Where to start! Phew!

What your English teacher is trying to do is get you to help the reader out. It's easy to forget when you're writing, and the story's really clear in your head, that the reader can't see the story happening as you can.

Metaphors and similes are good for this. They mean roughly the same thing; you're using a comparison to make things clearer. Let's say you want to describe a sinister man. You might decide the man should remind your reader of a toad. So, if you write,

"Webster was a toad of a man," you have used a metaphor; while if you write,

"Webster sat in the middle of the floor like a toad", you have used a simile. A simile has words like "as" or "like" in it.

Metaphors and similes can be very useful, but don't overdo them! They can get very complicated and choke up the whole story if you don't treat them with care.

Write on!

On my last essay my English teacher wrote, "appeal to the senses" and "be economical". Is she weird or what?

Dame Jennifer replies:
No, she isn't weird. What she means is that a person reading your story should be able to see, feel, hear and believe your impression as if he or she were part of the story. How else can the reader stay interested? You can

help the reader by mentioning in the story what things smell or taste like; what your characters see and hear; and what they can touch. By "be economical", your teacher means that you shouldn't rabbit on for hours about unimportant things. Instead, you should say, what is the one thing that makes me think that this is man is ugly, that this dog is funny, or that street is spooky? You can't do this unless you learn to observe people and things.

Write on!

I'm never sure how much to tell the reader. My teacher says I try too hard to describe everything in my stories so they get very long and boring, but if I don't tell the reader everything I'm worried that nobody will understand the story.

Dame Jennifer replies:

Don't worry! You can't do it all for the reader and it's pointless to try. A reader who isn't prepared to put some effort into reading your story isn't worth bothering about. Of course, you should give the reader all the help you can, but you have to trust readers to use their imaginations, too. Always keep the reader in mind while writing, but remember that creative writing needs creative reading!

Write on!

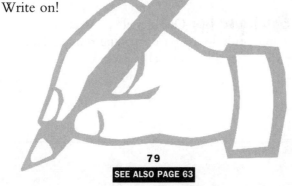

SEE ALSO PAGE 63

SPELLING AND OUTLINES

Develop Super Spelling Skills
with our once-a-day
Spelling Exercise Programme.

With **S.E.P** you can up your grades on your exams by filling out the weighting (additional marks) given for good spelling. Our weight-lifting programme is designed with you in mind, and your personal trainer, *I. Write Right*, will take you through her super steps to success.

1. Don't overdo it: Only pick one or two words per week to include in your personal plan, otherwise you'll stress out.

2. Stick to the plan: SEP only works if you keep at it. Give yourself a break on holidays, but otherwise work out every day.

3. Don't give up: Occasionally, a word won't stick and you'll lose a bit of spelling muscle. Keep working at it and you'll get it back.

Spelling Exercise Programme.

Set Up:
Have a sheet of paper marked out in columns. Have a pencil and eraser handy.

1. COPY Select a word that you often misspell and copy it correctly in the left-hand column in joined-up writing.

2. LOOK Look at the word and try to spell it in your head.

3. COVER Cover the word with a white piece of paper.

4. REMEMBER Try to picture the word on the white piece of paper.

5. WRITE Write the word, in joined-up writing, in the second column.

6. CHECK Make sure that the word is written correctly. If not, rub it out and repeat steps 2-6.

7. REPEAT Repeat steps 2-7 in columns 3, 4 and 5.

Add one or two words per week to the list, and keep on exercising those words until they are part of your spelling muscle power.

GET BETTER GRADES

COPY	1ST TRY	2ND TRY	3RD TRY	10 MINS LATER	NEXT WEEK	NEXT WEEK

Our resident art critic, Astabe Finicky, has been to the Graphi and Graphi collection of modern calligraphy to review the exhibition of Ille Gible's current style.

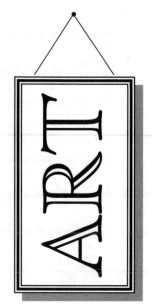

———◆———

Although the content of his work was striking in its originality, the quality didn't shine through because of his awful presentation. He has been reminded of his weaknesses by countless critics, but comments that his writing is "messy", "untidy" or "immature" haven't improved his writing style.

———◆———

In viewing Gible's work, we were able to spot the following problems:

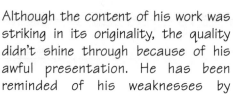

Here we see an obsession with modern transport, particularly with submarines and hovercrafts. His work seems to sink below the line or rise way above it.

The quick brown fox jumps over the lazy dog

Moving along, we see an awkward, cramped style with letters all the same height.

The quick brow

Finally we see Gible reverting to his pre-adolescent writing days, with huge letters, indicating a lack of artistic maturity.

If Gible were to focus on ONE error at a time, sort this problem out and then go on to the next one, his style would improve dramatically. In a very short time the style would truly reflect his unquestionable genius.

Unfortunately, as his writing is so slow, Gible produces only one piece a year. If he would get back to the practice of writing out the sentence:

The quick brown fox jumps over the lazy dog

(note that it cleverly contains every letter of the alphabet) Gible would soon get his speed in writing it down to under twenty seconds – a good standard for speed writing.

Of course, Gible would have to practise the sentence whilst keeping in mind the above criticisms (no transport obsessions, please, Gible), but his output would increase enormously.

And surely, if this is a lesson for Gible to learn, *we would all benefit from such advice!*

DIY

Better Grades own Do-It-Yourself expert, Percy Guzzard, helps sort out your problems with those final professional touches to make your writing make the grade!

So you've finished the essay, you think it's good: do you leave it as it is and hand it in? Of course not!

Now's the time to sort out any botches that may have crept into your beautifully constructed essay. Time to clean up the rough edges, smooth over the cracks, and turn it into the perfect job!

85

TOOLS:

1. Ink eradicator
2. Correcting pen
3. A list of DIY hints. These can be taken from the bottom of previously marked essays (the comments written by your teacher that you sometimes glance at, ignore and completely forget!).

TIME REQUIRED

As long as it takes to get your best results.
(In an exam, you should leave at least five minutes for each essay.)

Step 1: Read over your essay backwards (from the end to the beginning) to spot your spelling mistakes or words you don't think look "quite right".

Step 2: Ask someone for the correct spellings, or look them up in a dictionary. In an exam, try to improve on the original mistake.

Step 3: Read over your essay from the beginning using your list of DIY hints taken from previous work. In an exam, try to remember YOUR particular writing faults.

DIY PRACTICE

Read the next two paragraphs, have a good laugh and then see if you can find five spelling mistakes. Correct them on a separate piece of paper.

 Remember to read over the paragraphs **FROM** the **END** to the **BEGINNING**.

A man opened his door one evening to discover a seven-foot tall grasshopper standing on his doorstep. When the man asked what the insect wanted, the creachure swore at him, hit him over the head, kicked him to the ground and ran off, laughing hystericaly.

The man draged himself to the police station and told an officer of his harowing ordeal. The policeman listened patiently to the improbable tale and replied saying, "Yes sir, yours is not the first complaint of this nature that we have recieved this evening. It seems there's a nasty bug going round!"

ANSWERS ON PAGE 88

REVISION

Better Grades
QUIZ

Learn these facts in just two days and then answer the questions on the opposite page. How many can you get right?

1. The capital of France is Paris.
2. A thermistor is a device in which electrical resistance falls as temperature rises.
3. *Mare and Foals by a River* was painted by George Stubbs.
4. The feature film *Snow White* was produced by Walt Disney.
5. The capital of Pakistan is Islamabad.
6. Wool is produced from the coats of sheep.
7. The Battle of Holme was fought in 902.
8. A cartographer produces maps.
9. Ethology is the study of animal behaviour in the wild.
10. Swatch is the best selling Swiss watch.

How many items do you have to learn from this list? All ten? Wrong! It's more than likely that you already know some of these facts. Therefore you won't have to spend time learning all of them, because you only have to study what you don't know!

We spend far too much time on comfort study – going over material that we are already sure of and putting off learning what we don't know.

Answer the questions on the opposite page. You'll only have had to learn about half the facts.

DIY ANSWERS: Creature Hysterically Dragged Harrowing Received

1. What is the capital of France?

2. What is a thermistor?

3. Who painted *Mare and Foals by a River*?

4. Who produced the film *Snow White*?

5. What is the capital of Pakistan?

6. What does wool come from?

7. When was the Battle of Holme fought?

8. What do you call a person who produces maps?

9. What is the study of animal behaviour in the wild called?

10. What is the most popular brand of Swiss watch?

The Better Grades Famous Scientist* claims:

We remember
20 per cent of what we read,
30 per cent of what we hear,
40 per cent of what we see,
50 per cent of what we say,
60 per cent of what we do
AND 90 per cent of what we see, hear, say and do!

Therefore it is best if we are trying to memorise things to take an active approach to learning, not just sit back. Therefore, we recommend that you get a trainspotter's memory!

* Not the same one as before.

THE TRAINSPOTTING SPOT!

YES,

YOU CAN HAVE A

MEMORY LIKE A

TRAINSPOTTER!

Ever met a trainspotter?

They can usually be found on railway station platforms waiting for the 15.22 from Crewe and hoping that it's going to be a class 89 locomotive pulling ten mark 3 air-braked intercity coaches.

They wear anoraks and can be seen holding thermos flasks, sandwich boxes and notebooks. (Although the more sophisticated ones will have a Dictaphone.)

Okay so they may look a bit dull and can appear somewhat eccentric, but have you ever spoken to one?

You have? Okay, speaking to a trainspotter MAY be dull and can also be eccentric BUT try out this question.

Where did you see the class 47 "North Star" (or some other such locomotive)?

The most amazing thing is that they will almost definitely be able to tell you!

"Ah yes it was on Leicester station at 11.04 on March 2nd 1987. The weather was cold with a touch of rain in the air. The train arrived six minutes late due to a faulty signal box at Kettering. The train was pulling seven carriages and there wasn't a buffet car ... "

At this point tell them to shut up or just walk away, otherwise you will be told the life history of the engine, its carriages and the bacon sandwich served earlier.

The point is that trainspotters tend to have incredible memories for trains. (Try asking them a normal question like: "What's the highest mountain in the World?" and they may not be able to tell you as it hasn't got anything to do with trains.)

BUT why?

Well the most likely answer is that they remember the whole EXPERIENCE of spotting. They use all their senses: the smells, sights, sounds, the feel of the weather, the taste of the food whilst waiting for the train. It is a whole experience – an emotional thing! This is important because memory is linked to our emotions.

Add to this the fact that trainspotters are FOCUSED and INTERESTED in their chosen subject, and it's no wonder that they can remember the tiniest details.

THE *Better Grades* GUIDE TO
MEMORY TECHNIQUES!

BAD NEWS!

We forget 40 per cent of what we learn within five minutes!

70 per cent of everything you learn will be forgotten by tomorrow!

DON'T WORRY THOUGH!

This loss can be retrieved!

In order to use your memory effectively, you should start by looking at your own learning style.

How do YOU memorise successfully?

LEARNING STYLE	TRY
By creating visual images?	Drawing diagrams or pictures. highlight or underline text. Try to make a mental picture.
By repeating?	Read important points aloud. Explain to someone else.
By looking and copying?	Make notes on index cards.
By looking at old knowledge and linking the new to the old?	Brain Frames.

All these and many more are good practices. When you have discovered what works for you, go through the things that have to be memorised in all your subjects. See if it works for you!

SEE ALSO PAGE 57

MORE METHODS OF MEMORY

Rhyme and rhythm are particularly useful for remembering poetry, and sequencing tasks such as learning the alphabet or counting in a foreign language. Inventing poems about your subjects may help you to remember them. Actors find it easier to remember lines that rhyme than those that don't! You might even try writing a jingle or a song to help you remember the facts!

E.g. Here is a poem to remember the kings and queens of England:

Willy, Willy, Harry, Ste,
Harry, Dick, John, Harry three,
One, two, three Neds, Richard two,
Henry four, five, six then who?
Edward the fourth and Dick the Bad,
Henry twice and Ned the Lad,
Mary, Bessy, James the Vain,
Charlie, Charlie, James again,
William and Mary, Anne Gloria,
Then four Georges, William and Victoria,
Edward the seventh and George the fifth,
Edward the Eighth and George the Sixth...

...And Elizabeth

Mnemonics: These are excellent for helping you to remember! You probably know some already... For instance, **R**ichard **O**f **Y**ork **G**ave **B**attle **I**n **V**ain helps you to remember the colours of the rainbow in order: Red, Orange, Yellow, Green, Blue, Indigo, Violet. By remembering the sentence you can work out the colours.

Try making up mnemonics for the key points you need to remember. It may be hard, but by trying it, your memory will be helped!

 Understanding: Never try to memorise something that you do not understand. It won't work. It is usually best to try and write out the information you need to remember IN YOUR OWN WORDS. This will help you to understand it fully.

Sort out the material that has to be memorised, sort out the material you don't understand, ask for help, and by the time you have achieved full understanding you will find the amount you thought you had to memorise has been halved!

 Making links: Remember that your brain appreciates the familiar. When you learn something new, try to work out how you can link it to something you already know.

E.g. Even if you don't speak or read French, it is certain that you know many French words! Here is a list of French words:

fruit   train   pardon   table   fascination   document

Spot anything similar? Of course, these are all identical to the English! You are using knowledge that you already have (i.e. the English words) and linking the fact that they are exactly the same in French!

 Visual images: If you are very good at making visual images try Brain Framing (see page 57), wall charts, colour coding and flow diagrams.

 Memory aides: There are many useful memory aides on the market. Some are as simple as keeping your homework diary up to date, and at the other end of the scale there are electronic organisers which can record a mass of information. Make lists of "things to do", review them and update them regularly. The mere fact of making a list, even if you lose it, will help you to memorise it. (Ask anyone who makes shopping lists and then leaves the list at home – it is not usually the disaster you might expect, as most of the items can be remembered as a result of writing the list in the first place!)

If you are a person who receives information most naturally when listening, rather than when reading, use a tape recorder.

Time: You have to make sure that you use your time effectively! If you are the sort of person who thinks "Oh good, no homework!" when a teacher gives you learning or reading tasks for homework, you may be in trouble later!

Natural ability is an advantage, but most tasks are successfully achieved by CAREFUL PLANNING AND WORK!

Place of work: Identify an area that is ideal for working. (In front of a switched-on TV is not a good place to study!) Be honest about how much noise and interruption you can tolerate without becoming distracted. You are far more likely to remember and understand when you are totally focused on the task.

Time of work: It has been suggested that before you go to sleep is a good time to memorise facts on the basis that your mind will be undistracted during the hours of sleep. See if this is true. Some people operate much better in the early morning. Which type of person are you?

Learn with friends: One of the best ways to know if you have learned and memorised a topic is to see if you can teach it to a friend. Try it! It can be fun and gets rid of boredom!

Boredom: Boredom is not conducive to good memory skills. If you are bored, have a break and look at your motivation sheet (see page 12). Then come back to the work and refocus by sitting up, argue out loud with the writer (you might get some funny stares!). Also try to re-write the material so it is more interesting (for you, anyway!).

 Categorisation: Remember your brain is like a library. You need to file facts in the right place. This means linking new facts with old facts. Take your topic, and reduce it into smaller and smaller units. (Index cards can be very useful for this purpose.) This will help you to write down only the key words which will then trigger the memory.

 Vocabulary: You can't overload your poor memory by trying to learn twenty sections of your textbook two days before the exam. Repeating foreign words aloud helps your pronunciation, and imagery and association help your understanding of the meaning.

TOP TIP FOR LEARNING VOCABULARY

Take four words at a time, test word one, retest immediately, introduce word two, repeat and go back to word one, etc.

 Test yourself: By testing yourself and asking yourself whether you have understood your work, you are showing that you are memorising it!

 Evaluation: If you think about what you have learnt and how you have learnt it, you will soon be able to spot which methods of working are best for you. Remember everyone has a different learning style that will suit themselves. What works for someone else may not work for you. Find out what is the best way of learning for you! Be careful that you are not just learning parrot-fashion – it is important to UNDERSTAND what you are learning.

SEE ALSO PAGE 11

PLANNING YOUR TIME

DIPPY DAVE'S DAY

10 a.m. Got up. (I didn't get to bed until 3 as I was watching a late-night film.) Lay in bath.

11.00 a.m. Read paper and had coffee – thought about doing work.

12.00 a.m. Started biology revision.

12.01 a.m. Nipped to the shops for some milk.

12.30 p.m. Got home and made lunch.

1.00 p.m. Watched news.

1.30 p.m. Watched Australian soap.

2.00 p.m. Went up to room to revise, listened to records first.

3.00 p.m. Began to revise biology.

3.02 p.m. Remembered that I'd left the biology book that I needed at John's.

3.04 p.m. Went to John's. Chatted and listened to the latest BRAINCELL DEAD album. Then played ALLEY FIGHTER computer game. Lost. Damn!

5.14 p.m. Left John's.

5.30 p.m. Got home. Went to revise. Remembered that I'd forgotten to ask John for the book I'd gone to get! Decided to revise biology tomorrow.

5.40 p.m. Watched Australian soap.

6.00 p.m. Dinner.

6.30 p.m. Went out to play football at sports centre.

9.00 p.m. Finished football and went back to John's to pick up biology book.

9.15 p.m. Played computer game again. WON!

10.30 p.m. Got back home. Grief from parents about being in late and not doing any work for my exams.

10.45 p.m. Remembered that I'd forgotten the book

again.

11.00 p.m. Started to revise history. Too tired for it.

11.10 p.m. Watched film.

1.30 a.m. Had early night. Need to remember to pick up book tomorrow...

TRIFFIC TERRY'S DAY

4.30 a.m. Woke up. Quick shower.

4.32 a.m. Down to work! Revising biology. Read biology book from cover to cover.

5.30 a.m. Finished biology book. Started French revision. (Had to be quiet so as not to wake up mum and dad.) Read French book and looked over notes.

6.30 a.m. Had cup of coffee.

6.33 a.m. Continued with French.

7.33 a.m. Read geography book.

11.00 a.m. Time for a coffee and a biscuit.

11.05 a.m. Read geography book again.

12.30 p.m. Lunch.

12.45 p.m. Read geography notes.

3.00 p.m. Took a break for a cup of tea.

3.05 p.m. Back to geography book.

5.00 p.m. Made some notes on geography.

6.00 p.m. Dinner.

6.30 p.m. Read physics book.

9.00 p.m. Read physics notes.

11.00 p.m. Got ready for bed. Read physics book again.

12.00 p.m. Set alarm for 4.30 a.m. and went to sleep

So who is the ideal student, Dave or Terry? List your reasons on a piece of paper. Turn over for the answer.

Correct answer – NEITHER Dave nor Terry is an ideal student. The reason is that they do not use their time effectively!

Some of the reasons you may have spotted:

Dave
gets up late,
never gets down to work,
is disorganised (doesn't have his book available),
is easily distracted,
doesn't plan his time,
goes to bed late,
doesn't actually do any revision.

Terry
doesn't have enough sleep,
works ALL the time – no room for exercise, relaxation, etc.,
spends far too long working on one subject,
doesn't take enough breaks, hardly uses active learning techniques, he simply reads,
doesn't have a breakfast – it is important to get fuel into the body in order to produce energy. (If you were a car, you'd need fuel inside BEFORE setting off on a journey),
doesn't test himself on what he is reading – how does he know he's learnt anything?
doesn't revise with other people.

So it is important to have a balanced view towards studying. You can allow yourself leisure time, time for you to do what you want – exercise, watch TV, go to a party, see friends, etc. BUT it must be placed into a whole timetable! So use the Better Grades Weekly Planner to plan your time out.

WEEKLY REVISION AND HOMEWORK PLANNER

Make a copy of the plan over the page (you could photocopy this one if you have access to a photocopier with an enlarging facility).

Fill in exercise time and relaxation time.

Fill in family commitments (e.g. Grandmother's 60th birthday party etc.).

Then plan out what subjects you need to study and when they should be studied.

If you do not have enough time in which to fit in all your study requirements, then look carefully at your social commitments and reduce them!

SEE ALSO PAGES 18,98

THINGS TO THINK ABOUT WHEN PLANNING A REVISION TIMETABLE

Weekdays and weekends in the holidays – use this time effectively rather than spending ALL of it hanging around the local park or watching videos at a friend's house.

Weekday evenings and weekends in term time – try to plan out your use of this time.

Decide which subjects you need to spend more time on – these will include subjects that are important to you. Subjects which you are good at might need less revision time.

Exams or course work? – some subjects may be more course work based and so need less time for revision.

Time – are you giving yourself enough time for revision and study?

Realism – plan your study and revision time realistically. Don't try to fit everything into one week or one night; it won't work! For instance, if you were learning foreign vocabulary, it's easier to learn one new word each day rather than 200 in one night!

IF IN DOUBT – ASK YOUR TEACHER!

SUN	SAT			FRI	THURS	WED	TUES	MON	
		9-11am							4-5pm
		11-1pm							5-6pm
		1-3pm							6-7pm
		3-5pm							7-8pm
		5-7pm							8-9pm
		7-9pm							9-10pm
		9-11pm							10-11pm

QUICK QUIZ

Which is the best form of revision?

1. Revise all your maths, then all your biology, then all your English, then all your geography, etc.
2. Revise some maths, then some biology, then some English, then some geography etc.

Answer below.

> **Answer:** Method 2 is by far the better.
> a) You won't get bored by spending all your time on one subject.
> b) People learn better if they break up their revision into smaller chunks – there are more beginnings and endings (see page 104).
> NB Be sure not to revise more than three subjects per day.

HAVE A BREAK AND LEARN MORE!

Do you have a short attention span?

Excuse me, you, yes, you; stop looking away and flicking over the pages of the book, I'm talking to you!

Do you have a short attention span?

Don't worry. Everyone does!

You can learn more by taking regular breaks in your study time.

FACT: After about half an hour, people's attention span flags and concentration drops off.

SO: Plan your study time in 30 – 40 minute sessions.

FACT: People remember more at the beginning and the end of a study session.

SO: After a break spend five to 10 minutes going over what you studied just before the break. This will mean that you have more "endings" and more "beginnings" in your period of study.

FACT: You are four times more likely to remember your notes when you constantly revise them.

SO: Look at them for a few minutes after an hour, then the next day, then the next week, then the next month.

LITTLE AND OFTEN
IS THE KEY!

SEE ALSO PAGES 90

EXAMS

The *Better Grades* Guide to Beating the Examiner!

1 Know exactly what the exam entails. It is **VITAL** that you know the answer to these questions:
How long does the exam last?
How many questions will you have to answer?
Do you have to write essays?
Are there multiple choice questions?

2 Look at copies of past exam papers. These will help you to get the "feel" of the exam and the type of question that may be asked.

3 Listen to teachers – they will be able to give you some idea of the types of questions that will be asked.

4 Imagine yourself as the examiner. What would you ask if you wanted to test someone's knowledge about the subject?

5 Create a group of you to forecast what questions might be asked. The more heads, the more questions you'll think of!

6 Prepare essays in advance. Make essay plans of the possible questions. Obviously you can't take them into the exam with you, but if you've already prepared them, you're more likely to remember them in the exam!

7 Practise writing essays to the set time limit you will have in the exam.

You might be lucky and some of the actual questions come up in the exam. If not, the practice of writing essays, revising with friends and preparing plans will be invaluable.

8 Use revision notes if they are of benefit to you.

---

20 Things you always wanted to know...

...about the person who marks your English GCSE exam paper.

1 How many papers do you mark each June?
Up to 500!

2 How long are you given to mark them?
3-4 weeks.

3 Approximately how much do you get paid per paper?
About enough to buy a pint of beer!

4 Do you enjoy marking papers?
Sometimes yes, sometimes NO!

5 Do you ever know whose paper you are marking?
I know the name but it would be very unlikely that I knew the person.

6 Do you deduct marks for poor handwriting?
Yes, a few.

7 How many marks do you deduct for bad spelling and poor punctuation?
The rules for deductions change year by year. Ask your teacher to check with your exam board.

8 Can you tell if a student has planned an essay?
Yes.

9 Should pupils show their plans?
Yes.

10 Do you look for "quantity" or "quality"?
Quality (although there is usually a minimum quantity).

11 What really annoys you about exam answers?
When students have not followed the rubric (instructions on the front sheet).

12 What really impresses you about exam answers?
Quality of knowledge, perception and personal response.

13 Do you find yourself liking or hating a student from his or her answers?
No.

14 How do you feel when you give a failing mark?
It is vital NOT to give any personal response – be neutral.

15 Have you ever suspected a student of cheating?
No.

16 How would you deal with cheating?
Report it to the team leader and send the paper to them.

17 How late do you stay up marking?
I try to stop myself marking after 10.30 p.m. so I'm not marking some papers when I'm tired.

18 What annoys you most about marking exams?
Time-scale and low pay!

19 Do you have to mark papers during your holidays?
Yes.

20 What job do you usually do?
I'm a teacher, although there are people who are retired teachers, lecturers; in fact, all sorts of people mark papers.

THE *Better Grades* FILM REVIEW
by Harry Boreman

FILM OF THE WEEK
The Twisted Examiner (Rated A – G)

THIS IS NOT A FILM FOR THE SQUEAMISH!

Ace Marx, faced with the constant threat of failure, manages, with the help of his Get Better Grades guide, to outwit the twisted examiner by using study skills and exam techniques.

He almost fails at the first hurdle when the examiner pressures him with limited time in order to tempt Ace into answering questions without reading all of them first.

With deft skill, Ace bravely stops to take a deep breath and reads all of the examination paper thoroughly. Ace gets into the examiner's sinister mind, imagining that HE is the evil examiner and asks himself, "What does Ace Marx have to do to get round my horrible questions?"

Just before delving into the exam whirlpool, Ace takes time to outline his answers, thus depriving the examiner of the pleasure of accusing him of leaving out any important facts. Finally Ace stuns the examiner by proof-reading his answers, correcting spelling mistakes and tying up the loose ends.

In the final scene, worthy of some of the greatest moments in World cinema (one is reminded of Spielberg, Tarantino and Walt Disney) the examiner is forced to give Ace an A grade, before he is dragged away screaming to the Home for Maniacal Markers.

A great film that has something for all students about to take exams. Catch it!

Exams Aagghhhhhhh!!!!!

Exams are a stressful time in your life.
What is there to worry about? **LOTS!**

☞ pressure of revision
☞ fear of failure
☞ parental pressure
☞ wanting to get a job

Yes, plenty you can get stressed about. The following can be signs of stress:

I can't remember a thing.

I don't feel in control.

There's too much to do.

I can't do exams. I'll never pass.

I have real feelings of panic.

I can't get round to doing any work.

THERE'S NOTHING WRONG WITH ME, OKAY! AND I'M NOT IRRITABLE RIGHT? RIGHT!!!!?

Everyone is better than I am, they'll all do better than me!

But you can beat exam stress by following Better Grades resident psychiatrist, Sigmund Fraud's Stress Beater Plan:

1 Try to identify exactly why you may be worried. It could be that you have only one or two weak areas. By identifying your strengths and weaknesses you can get things into a better perspective.

2 Talk about any worries you have with friends, teachers or your parents. They may well be able to offer good advice and will be able to give you different viewpoints on your difficulties. Remember, a problem shared is a problem halved!

3 Make sure that you have an organised plan of revision. By knowing what you have to do and when, tasks will seem more manageable and you'll be less likely to get stressed.

4 Try to take some form of relaxation – breathing exercises are excellent for this! Make sure that you don't spend ALL your time studying. Leave some time for relaxation – playing sport, listening to music or watching television are all good ways of relaxing and taking your mind off the exams!

5 Make sure that you get a good night's sleep – eight hours is the average. Resting will help reduce the stress. It's also important to eat a balanced diet and avoid coffee!

FINALLY
Remember not to take everything too seriously! Although it feels bad not to do as well as you had hoped in an exam, it ISN'T a life or death situation! Keep things in perspective!

SEE ALSO PAGES 98,101

BEFORE THE EXAM

1 Make sure you know which day your exam is on!

2 Know what time the exam starts! Make sure you arrive in good time – if using public transport, set off earlier than usual to make sure you're on time!

3 Know where the exam takes place. Visit the exam room before the exam in order to familiarise yourself with the surroundings.

4 Make sure you've eaten well before an exam – carbohydrates are a good source of energy (perhaps take a snack bar into the exam to nibble on if you're feeling drained – check that you would be allowed to do this).

5 Try to relax! Easier said than done, but you need to feel slightly nervous before an exam in order to be at your best! Use deep-breathing exercises to get oxygen into your brain. You may have other techniques for helping you to relax, but remember NO alcohol or drugs before an exam. These will stop you performing to your potential.

The night before an exam is a good time to spend some time relaxing. Sit in front of the TV, watch a funny video or read a "light" book. This will certainly help.

Check that you've got your equipment for the exam as well, this will stop you panicking in the morning.

6 Get a good night's sleep!

7 On the morning of the exam get up half an hour earlier than you normally do. This will give you plenty of time to sort yourself out, and not become stressed by rushing around.

SITTING EXAMS

QUESTION:

You're sitting in the exam room. You're nervous (so is everyone else!). What do you do now to make sure you do yourself justice in the exam?

ANSWER:

Follow the *Better Grades* guide to sitting exams.

- ☞ Keep calm.
- ☞ Listen to the invigilator's instructions.
- ☞ Check that you have the correct exam paper.
- ☞ Read the instructions carefully. Note how many questions you have to answer and how many are compulsory.
- ☞ Fill in all your details carefully (name, number, etc).
- ☞ Read through **ALL** of the exam paper.
- ☞ Tick the questions you choose to answer.
- ☞ Read the questions carefully, making sure you understand them. Underline key words in the question to help you do this. (See also page 133).
- ☞ Divide the time up between the questions. Give more time to those questions that award more marks. Leave time for checking at the end.
- ☞ Answer the question that you feel you will answer best **FIRST**. This will help to put you into a confident mood.
- ☞ **PLAN** your answer. Write down, in rough, any ideas that spring to mind or formulae you may wish to use. Stick to answering what the question is asking you.
- ☞ Write the answer.

☞ Check your answer against your plan – have you missed anything out?

☞ Proof-read your answer, checking that it is legible, punctuation is used correctly and spellings are correct.

☞ Repeat this procedure until you have completed every question you have to answer.

☞ Check through all of your answers.

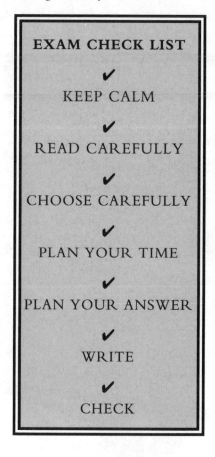

EXAM CHECK LIST

✔

KEEP CALM

✔

READ CAREFULLY

✔

CHOOSE CAREFULLY

✔

PLAN YOUR TIME

✔

PLAN YOUR ANSWER

✔

WRITE

✔

CHECK

DEAR BRENDA

Dear Brenda,
I am about to take my exams and am worried sick about them. Lots of crazy questions are running round my head and I can't seem to figure out the answers, can you help? For instance: what happens if I run out of time in the exam before I've finished the questions? What happens if I need to go to the toilet? What if Ann or Jim or any of my mates try to talk to me during the exam? Also, should I discuss the exam with anyone when I've finished it?
Please help me: I know these questions are silly, but they're driving me CRAZY!
Ian Sane

SEE ALSO PAGE 118

Dear Ian,

Of course your questions are not silly, they're commonplace and the sort of thing students do worry about. Exam time is, I'm afraid, a stressful time and little questions seem to be vitally important.

Anyway, to try to answer your questions. If you find yourself running out of time, briefly summarise what you intended to write if you had the time. You are more likely to get more marks for two summary answers rather than a full one. In maths, it is important to show working out (you may get some marks, even if your answer is wrong).

If you need to go to the toilet, raise your hand and wait for the invigilator to arrive and explain the situation (oh yes, and try to have gone BEFORE the exam!).

If your friends try to talk to you during the exam, you MUST ignore them. Otherwise you may well pay the ultimate sanction and be thrown out of the exam.

Finally, after you have finished the exam remember that it is over and you can't do anything about it, so perhaps it is advisable not to talk to anyone about it, rather you should start to think positively about the next one.

Good luck!

Brenda

THE EXAM GAME

START

1 Arrive late
PANIC!

2

3 Read all questions carefully
Advance 3 spaces

4 Forgot to have breakfast
Miss a turn

7

6

5 Feel confident as you've revised well
Have another turn

8 Work out how long you have for each question
Miss a turn

9 Forgot your glasses
PANIC!

10

11 Accidentally brought a book in to the exam
Return to start

12

15

14 Brought all equipment into exam
Have another turn

13 Didn't revise a particular question
PANIC!

16 Daydreaming
Miss 2 turns

17 Forgot to go to the toilet before the exam started
Miss a turn

18

19

20 Answered the easiest question first
Advance 2 spaces

118

WELL DONE!
FINISH

38 Leave enough time to check through all your answers
Have another go

39

40 Don't have time to check work
Miss a turn

37 Speak to a fellow student
THROWN OUT! YOU LOSE!

36 Take care over your spelling and punctuation
Have another go

35

34 Spend 10 mins on a question worth 40 marks and 20 mins on a question worth 10
Go back 7 spaces

33 Finished exam Still an hour to go
Go back to the start for not planning properly

30 Running out of time
PANIC!

31 Draw a clear diagram to support your answer
Advance 2 spaces

32

29 Proof read your essay
Have another turn

28

27

26 FOUND CHEATING
THROWN OUT! YOU LOSE!

25

22

23 Spend some time making an essay outline
Advance 4 spaces

24 Answered the wrong question
PANIC!

21 Pen runs out. You don't have another one
PANIC!

119

PANIC! BOX

To play the exam game you need:
❏ a die (*just one dice, silly!*)
❏ a counter for each player (*any number can play*).

You may wish to photocopy the gameboard before playing.

RULES

1. Players take it in turns to throw the die and move their counter.

2. Follow the instructions when landing on a square.

3. If you land on a Panic! square, place your counter in the Panic! box. You must throw an even number before you can return to the Panic! square you came from.

4. If you land on **THROWN OUT** you have lost!

The winner is the first to reach the end!
(*If only real exams were this easy!!*)

❏ NOW READ THE NEXT PAGE CAREFULLY AND ANSWER THE QUESTIONS ON PAGE 122.

Better Grades EXAM BORED

GCSE
SUBJECT: GENERAL STUDIES
Paper 2

Thursday 15th June 1997 1.30 p.m.-4.00 p.m.
Two and a half hours.

There are three sections. You should spend approximately half an hour on section 1, and approximately an hour each on sections 2 and 3.

Write your name and number in the box at the top of each page and also the answer sheet.
Read all questions before answering.

Section 1 (20%): Multiple choice
Answer all 20 questions in section 1. There are four possible answers. Use an HB pencil to shade in the correct number on the answer sheet provided. Rub out your answer if you change your mind. Do not use a pen.

Section 2 (40%)
This section is divided into A and B. Answer three questions in this section. You must answer at least one question from section A and at least one from section B.
   Use a new sheet of paper to start each question.

Section 3 (40%)
Answer both questions. You may use diagrams to illustrate your answer.

You will be supplied with   :   an exam paper
                                   an answer sheet for section 1
                                   an answer booklet for sections
                                   2 and 3
                                   an HB pencil
You may use a calculator.
The use of dictionaries or correcting fluid is not permitted.

Marks may be lost for poor English and presentation.

BREAK THE CODE
Exams have a language of their own!

Unfortunately, year after year many students don't break the code and lose marks because they haven't followed the instructions (the rubric). It has been estimated that poor reading of exam papers was responsible for two thirds of all "silly" mistakes made by students! Read the Better Grades Rubric then answer the following questions and break the code!

1. What subject is being examined?
2. How many questions in total do you have to answer?
3. How long is the exam?
4. How many compulsory questions do you have to answer in Section 2 B?
5. What equipment should you take into the exam?
6. How long should you allocate to answering each question in Section 3?
7. What is meant by multiple choice questions?
8. What advice is offered?
9. What are you not allowed to take in to the exam?
10. What is the most important instruction on the paper?

BETTER GRADES TOP TIP

When looking at an exam paper, make sure that you <u>underline</u> or highlight key words. Re-read questions BEFORE beginning to answer.

BREAK THE CODE
Answers

1. GCSE General Studies.
2. 25 (20 in section 1, three in section 2 and two in section 3).
3. 2 1/2 hours.
4. At least one.
5. Pens, eraser, pencils, rulers, calculator (and a spare battery for the calculator in case it runs out in the exam!).
6. 30 minutes to each question.
7. You will be offered a choice of four answers, one of which is correct.
8. How much time you should allocate to each section, use diagrams in section 3, use calculators and be careful with both your use of English and presentation.
9. Dictionaries and correcting fluid.
10. Read all questions before answering.

SPEAK UP

Bonjour and hello! John Paul Goatee is here to help you with your French orals.

Maintenant, chers garçons et filles...
For those eemportant oral exhams you murst mack sheur that you are ready et able pour them. Ma ot tips eenclude:
(At this point we have had to translate John Paul into English that you can understand! – Editors.)

SPEAK UP

★Rehearse possible scenarios that could turn up.
★Speak in French to your family and friends.
(Okay, so they won't understand you, but what else is new!)
★Work with friends – tape each other having conversations so you can criticise your vocabulary, pronunciation and accent.
★Listen to French programmes on the TV and tune into French radio stations.
★Speak clearly in the exam.
★Listen closely to the questions. If you don't understand what the examiner is asking, ask them to repeat it. (If you still don't understand, tell the examiner that you are sorry, but you still don't understand it. They will either rephrase it or give you another question.)

★REMEMBER – the questions that the examiner asks you may well depend on answers that you have already given. Therefore you may well be able to steer the conversation round to topics in which you are confident!

BONNE CHANCE!
Of course these tips are good for any oral exam, be it English, German, Japanese, etc. etc!

Dear Brenda,
I am an examiner and I get very depressed and angry when students don't spell words correctly in their exams. Can you help me?
From
Anne Xaminer

Dear Anne,
Yes, I can. I've got the writers of this book to print a list of words that are commonly misspelt by students in exams. These can be found on page 129. Hopefully everyone that reads this book will take note of them, learn the spellings that give them trouble and when they sit their exams they won't make you angry and depressed by spelling them incorrectly!
Brenda

Dear Brenda,
I am also an examiner and I get MAD with students who spell words incorrectly even when the words are actually ON the exam paper.
What can I do?
N Uther-Xaminer
(Mr)

Dear Mr Uther-Xaminer,
I am afraid that I can't help you. It's up to the students to read the exam paper carefully and check out spellings. They could also proof-read their answers when they have finished writing them. Unfortunately, I can't really help you. Sorry.
Brenda

REFERENCE SECTION

STAGE 1

Better Gr

Identify your weakness.

You may be a weak speller in one of the following ways:

1. You can't spell the **specialist vocabulary** you need for a particular subject, e.g. *Mediterranean* or *apparatus*.

2. You make **"silly" mistakes** which you can correct yourself when they are pointed out e.g. *thay/makeing*.

3. You really do have a **problem** with spelling – you haven't a clue if *cat/kat, fraction/fracshun* is correct.

STAGE 2

Select a sample of twenty words which have been misspelled in your writing books.

STAGE 3

Which one of these methods would appeal to you the most?

ABCDEFGHIJKLMOPQRSTUVWXYZ
abcdefghijklmnopqrstuvwxyz

▶▶ The multi-sensory approach:

You get the word into your brain by using all your *senses* – that means you *write* it, you *say* it, you *listen* to what you have said and you *look* at it. Choose a word a day and practise that word every day for a week. (See LOOK, COVER, WRITE, CHECK).

SEE ALSO PAGE 80

▶▶ The spelling rule approach:

You find it helpful to know *why* a word is spelled in a particular way. For example, here is a spelling rule:

Make the sound *k* as in *cat*. There are four ways of spelling that sound:

➤ At the beginning of the word: always with a C unless the next letter is E or I, e.g. cat, crafty, clever, chair – BUT K*en* and K*it*.

➤ At the end of a short word (one syllable) you have to make a choice of using *k* or *ck*. Use *ck* if it comes immediately after a vowel which makes its sound, e.g. pa*ck* thi*ck* so*ck*s, BUT thi*nk* da*rk* mi*lk*.

➤ When you hear *k* at the end of a longer word you always spell it with a *c* e.g. fantasti*c* picni*c*.

➤ Finally, sometimes *k* is spelled with a *ch* as in chemist, chronic and chrome. You just have to recognise those ones.

ABCDEFGHIJKLMOPQRSTUVWXYZ
abcdefghijklmnopqrstuvwxyz

Here is a more complicatd rule for **shun** as in station:

The electri **cian** went to the sta **tion** and then on to collect his pen **sion**. Can you work it out?

cian = anything to do with jobs, e.g. politi**cian**, mathemati**cian**, magi**cian**. The **an** stands for man eg magic man – too bad if you're female!

Otherwise if you hear **shun** always spell it with **tion** UNLESS the letter before is L, N, R or S. (You can use the mnemonic "Lovely Naughy Rude Songs".) So it's section, fraction, BUT repulsion, mansion, immersion, succession.

If you like that intellectual method buy yourself a good spelling textbook and go for it. There are exceptions but you will learn more than five words a week!

▶▶▶▶ The auditory approach and the visual approach:

If you know you only receive information through your ears or your eyes, stick every word you need on posters all over your room if you are a visual person; and if you are an auditory (listening) person get yourself a tape and repeat the spellings over the tape. Get people to test you in both cases.

▶▶▶▶ The dealing with "silly mistakes" approach:

If you make silly mistakes which you know you can correct then you need to use the proof-reading technique (see page 85).

FINALLY, improving your spelling takes some effort – get people to help you, focus on your problem.

Better Grades
WORST EVER WORDS FOR SPELLING

always	any	answer	ache
almost	again	across	around
already	business	beginning	believe
because	buy	built	chose
choose	cough	county	course
colour	don't	doctor	duly
except	forty	fourth	friend
government	grammar	guess	hear
here	how	its	it's
instead	knew	lose	loose
many	meant	new	necessary
often	off	of	parliament
peace	piece	quite	quiet
receive	sincerely	some	sure
separate	sugar	straight	they
too	to	their	there
through	tough	thought	though
trouble	which	witch	who
when	what	where	wear
were	whole	why	write
whether	weather	wholly	whose

DAYS OF THE WEEK
Monday, Tuesday, Wednesday, Thursday, Friday,
Saturday, Sunday

MONTHS OF THE YEAR
January, February, March, April, May, June, July,
August, September, October, November, December

Better Grades
PUNCTUATION POINTERS

There are several easy-to-use books which will show you how to punctuate your essays correctly. If you are being criticised for poor punctuation, **BUY ONE!**

The following is a quick reference guide to some of the uses of three frequently employed punctuation marks, and one which is seldom used.

CAPITAL LETTERS

Used at the beginning of sentences:

Go upstairs and do your homework.

Why do I always have to sit in the middle of the back row?

Used for names of people (Percy), institutions (Disneyland), days (Monday), months (January), holidays (Christmas), countries (Pakistan), cities (Gotham), states (~~Masachusits~~, ~~Massichusus~~, ~~Massachussi~~, Texas), counties (Surrey), provinces (Quebec), towns (Northampton), villages (Boring by the Sea), languages (French), religions (Christianity), titles of people (Bishop Shepherd), and titles of books, magazines, plays, poems and programmes (*Happy Days, The Shoe Programme, The Joys of Typing*).

Most common mistake:
Using capital letters in the middle of sentences to indicate an important word: (I Really like ice cream.)

Better Grades Pointer:

If you think you have trouble with full stops and capital letters, think out a sentence completely before committing it to paper. After you have written it down, put your pen down and think of the next sentence.

COMMAS

Used to separate items in a list:
Yesterday I bought a pack of gum, a new disk, some sweets for my cousin, and a crocodile for my brother.

Used to set apart groups of words that need to show themselves as separate descriptions, or additions, to the main theme of the sentence:
My friend Lucy, who is one of the most exciting people I know, is keen on trainspotting. Another of her hobbies is flower pressing, a truly thrilling pastime.

Used before direct speech, and to separate direct speech from the rest of the sentence:
Bert said, "I know a great place where we can watch snails racing."

"I've got a great idea," I said. "Let's get Bert and Lucy together for a date."

Notice that the commas go INSIDE the speech marks.

Most common mistake:
Using commas like confetti and throwing them around a sentence needlessly.

Better Grades Pointer:
When in doubt, leave them out.

APOSTROPHES

Used to show possession:
John's trendy shoes, John's faded jeans, John's baseball cap.

Used to contract two words into one:
John's (John is) a poser.

Most common mistake:
Using apostrophes for plurals - six stick's, fish and chip's.

Better Grades Pointer:
Avoid using contractions in formal writing.

SEMI-COLONS

Used to separate two closely related themes in a sentence.
"Bert and Lucy are getting married; a banjo band will be playing at their wedding."

Most common mistake:
Being afraid to use a semi-colon for fear of getting it wrong.

Better Grades Pointer:
Try to use the occasional semi-colon in your writing; using it with 'however' or 'on the other hand' can make it really easy.

"Bert and Lucy wanted to go to Slough for their honeymoon; however, they decided against it as they thought it would be too exciting."

KEY WORDS

What do those words mean in essay titles?

Account for
Explain. Examine the points that make up the subject you are being asked about.

Analyse
Explore the main ideas of the subject: show why they are important and how they are related.

Comment on
Discuss the subject, explain it and give an opinion on it.

Compare
Show the similarities (but you could also point out the differences).

Contrast
Show the differences ("Compare and Contrast" questions are very common in exams).

Criticise
Analyse and then make a judgement or an opinion. You should show both its good and its bad points. (You could refer to an expert's opinion within this question.)

Define
Give the meaning. This should be short and concise.

Describe
Give a detailed account. Attempt to make it as complete as possible by moving from an overview to a more

detailed examination of the subject.

Differentiate
Explore and explain the difference.

Discuss
Explore the subject by looking at its advantages and disadvantages (i.e. pros and cons, for and against). Attempt to come to some sort of judgement.

Distinguish
Explain the difference.

Evaluate
Give an opinion by exploring the merits of the subject. Look at the pros and cons. Attempt to support your argument with expert opinion.

Explain
Make it clear. How does it work? What is the underlying principle of the subject? Etc. Illustrate. Give clear examples.

Interpret
Explain the meaning by using examples and opinions.

Justify
Give good reasons for offering an opinion or reaching a conclusion.

List
Give the reasons or points one by one.

Outline
Give an overall view of the subject. Include main points and avoid minor details.

Prove
Support your argument by using facts, figures and examples.

Relate
Show the connections between things.

State
Present the main points in a clear, concise form.

Summarise
Give a brief account of the main points. Attempt to come to some conclusion of your own.

Trace
Describe how something has developed in its chronological order. Describe the causes and effects.

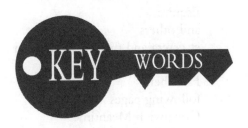

Better Grades
GUIDE TO ABBREVIATIONS & SYMBOLS

@	at
a/c	account
ad:	advertisement
a.d.:	after date
a.k.a.	also known as
a.m.	before noon (Latin – *ante meridiem*)
a.s.a.p.	as soon as possible
Ave.	Avenue
BC	Before Christ
BST	British Summer Time
c.	century
c. or ca.	around (Latin – *circa*)
cf.	compare
Co.	Company or County
c/o	care of
Dr	Doctor
E.	East
e.g.	for example (Latin – *exempli gratia*)
Esq.	Esquire
et al.	and others
etc.	et cetera and the rest, and so on
et seq.	and the following
F	Farenheit
ff	following pages
GMT	Greenwich Meantime
i.e.	that is (Latin – *id est*)
Inc.	incorporated
i.q.	*idem quod* (Latin – the same as)

l.c.	in the passage (Latin – *loco citato*)
Ltd.	limited
MS	manuscript or multiple sclerosis
N.	North
n/a	not applicable
NB	Take note or note well. This is important! (Latin – *nota bene*)
n.d.	no date
no.	number
nr.	near
o.n.o.	or nearest offer
p.	page
PA	personal assistant
p.a.	per annum (every year)
p. and p.	postage and packing
p.c.	per cent
pd.	paid
pl.	place or plural
p.m.	after noon (Latin – *post meridiem*)
pp.	pages
PS	postscript
PTO	please turn over
QED	which was to be demonstrated (Latin – *quod erat demonstrandum*)
q.v.	which see – found in references (Latin – *quod vide*)
qy	query
Rd.	road
RSVP	please reply (French – réspondez s'il vous plaît)
s.	second(s)
s.a.	without date (Latin – *sine anno*)
s.a.e.	stamped addressed envelope
Sec.	secretary

SCIENTIFIC TERMS

C	centigrade or celsius
cg	centigram(s)
c.p.	candlepower
c.p.s. or c/s	cycles per second
cu.	cubic
dB	decibel(s)
dl	decilitre(s)
dm	decimetre(s)
e.m.f.	electromotive force
g	gram(s)
gr.	grain or gross
h	hecto-
HF	high frequency
Hz	hertz
in.	inch(es)
i.p.s.	inch(es) per second
J	Joule
K	Kelvin
k	kilo-
kg.	kilogram(s)
kHz	kilohertz
k.p.h.	kilometres per hour
kV	kilovolt
kW	kilowatt
kWh	kilowatt-hour
lb	pounds (weight)
LCM	least common multiple
LF	low frequency
m.	metres or minutes
mg	milligram
MHz	megahertz
ml.	millilitres or miles
mm.	millimetre(s)

m.p.h.	miles per hour
MW	megawatt
oz.	ounce(s)
p.p.m.	parts per million
qr.	quarter
qt.	quart(s)
r.p.m.	revolutions per minute
sq.	square
t.	ton(s) or tonne(s)
UHF	ultra high frequency
UHT	ultra heat treated
UV	ultraviolet
V	volt
VDU	visual display unit
VHF	very high frequency
W	watt(s)

INDEX